Sustaining Social Security
in an Era of
Population Aging

Sustaining Social Security in an Era of Population Aging

John A. Turner

2016

WE focus
series

W.E. Upjohn Institute for Employment Research
Kalamazoo, Michigan

Library of Congress Cataloging-in-Publication Data

Names: Turner, John A. (John Andrew), 1949- author.
Title: Sustaining social security in an era of population aging / John A. Turner.
Description: Kalamazoo, Mich. : W.E. Upjohn Institute for Employment Research,
    2016. | Series: WE Focus series | Includes bibliographical references and index.
Identifiers: LCCN 2016032575 (print) | LCCN 2016038986 (ebook) | ISBN
    9780880995153 (pbk. : alk. paper) | ISBN 0880995157 (pbk. : alk. paper) |
    ISBN 9780880995160 (ebook) | ISBN 0880995165 (ebook)
Subjects: LCSH: Social security—United States. | Pension trusts—United States. |
    Pensions—United States. | Older people—Government policy—United States.
Classification: LCC HD7125 .T87 2016 (print) | LCC HD7125 (ebook) | DDC
    368.4/300973—dc23
LC record available at https://lccn.loc.gov/2016032575

The facts presented in this study and the observations and viewpoints expressed are the sole responsibility of the author. They do not necessarily represent positions of the W.E. Upjohn Institute for Employment Research.

Cover design by Carol A.S. Derks.
Index prepared by Diane Worden.
Printed in the United States of America.
Printed on recycled paper.

Contents

Tables

Acknowledgments

This book provides an introduction to how Social Security works and how it could be reformed to work better. Social Security is the foundation of our retirement income system and for the most part works well. However, it does not have sufficient funding to pay promised benefits starting around 2033. Also, it needs to be updated to reflect the large improvement in life expectancy that has occurred since the Social Security Act was signed by Franklin Delano Roosevelt in 1935.

I have benefited from previous collaborations with a number of scholars cited in the text, including Clive Bailey, David Blake, Ellen Bruce, Richard Burkhauser, Tianhong Chen, Yung-Ping Chen, Tabitha Doescher, Teresa Ghilarducci, Colin Gillion, Gerard Hughes, Mark Iwry, Bruce Klein, Rose Musonye Kwena, Denis Latulippe, Adelin Levin, Jules Lichtenstein, David McCarthy, Olivia Mitchell, Courtney Monk, Dana Muir, Leslie Muller, David Rajnes, Martin Rein, Adam Samborski, Sally Shen, Norman Stein, Marek Szczepański, Noriyasu Watanabe, and Natalia Zhivan. I have also benefited from comments on this manuscript by Kevin Hollenbeck and two anonymous reviewers.

Readers interested in this book may also be interested in the following books published by Upjohn Institute.

For a more detailed discussion of individual accounts for Social Security reform: *Individual Accounts for Social Security Reform: International Perspectives on the U.S. Debate* (Turner 2006).

For a discussion of pension policy: *Pension Policy: The Search for Better Solutions* (Turner 2010).

For a discussion of retirement income policy as it is affected by increasing longevity: *Longevity Policy: Facing Up to Longevity Issues Affecting Social Security, Pensions, and Older Workers* (Turner 2011).

For a discussion of retirement income system reform from an international perspective: *Imagining the Ideal Pension System: International Perspectives* (Muir and Turner 2011); *Social Security and Pension Reform: International Perspectives* (Szczepański and Turner 2014a).

Chapter 1

How Does Social Security Work?

The year 2015 marked the eightieth anniversary of Social Security.[1] The federal government spends more on Social Security than it does on any other single program—its outlays account for nearly a quarter of all federal spending (Meyerson and Dacey 2013). Social Security is arguably the most important social program in the United States, providing the main source of retirement income for most people. Its importance as a regular, reliable source of retirement income has increased in recent years with the decline in employer-provided defined benefit plans, which previously dominated the U.S. retirement income system. Over time, however, 401(k) plans have replaced them as the prevailing plan, and more recently, Individual Retirement Accounts (IRAs) have become the most important type of private-sector plan (Investment Company Institute 2015). Thus, people have a greater need for the insurance protection Social Security benefits provide, but changes already in place are reducing the generosity of its benefits for future retirees (Turner 2001; Weller 2016).

Yet Social Security is in need of reform. It does not have sufficient financing to pay promised benefits, and the option of maintaining the status quo is not feasible. In addition, with increases in longevity at older ages, reforms are needed to better target benefits to older persons. While there have been many proposals for Social Security reform, they generally are ad hoc in nature, meaning that they do not address the fundamental financing problem.

As demonstrated later in this book, the fundamental problem is that in the current demographic era where the old-age dependency ratio (the ratio of Social Security beneficiaries to covered workers) is increasing, the Social Security benefit formula causes benefits to grow faster than the tax revenues that finance them. Thus, while the problem can be viewed as one of demographics (which is a problem that cannot be fixed), I argue that the problem is the structure of the benefit formula. Although ad hoc reforms have a place, they do not fundamentally restore Social Security to solvency. The current Social Security benefit formula is not financially sustainable in the long run without periodic reforms.

Technically, the solutions for fixing Social Security are easy, but the reality is that politically fixing Social Security is a difficult, complex problem. This book tackles the political problem.

Social Security reform can involve a major change to its structure or it can involve adjustments to the levels of key parameters in the current structure. Thus, a distinction can be made between paradigmatic reform versus parametric reform. Paradigmatic reform would involve a major change in the fundamental structure of Social Security, such as by introducing individual accounts. President George W. Bush attempted paradigmatic reform by introducing individual accounts, but that effort met fierce opposition and ultimately was dropped. Parametric reform involves changing the value of the parameters of the system without changing the structure, such as raising the tax rate that finances benefits or reducing the generosity of benefits. Parametric reform usually involves relatively small changes to the basic parameters of the Social Security system—the payroll tax rate, the maximum level of earnings subject to the payroll tax, the generosity of benefits, the cost-of-living indexing of benefits in payment, and the age at which benefits can be received. Social Security reform in the United States traditionally has been parametric reform.

In addition to the division between paradigmatic reform and parametric reform, a new category of reform can be called extreme parametric reform. Whereas parametric reform involves relatively small changes in the parameters of Social Security, extreme parametric reform involves dramatic changes. An example is Vermont Senator and 2016 presidential candidate Bernie Sanders's Social Security proposal, which would subject all income, not just labor market income, above $250,000 to the Social Security payroll tax (Backman 2016).

SCOPE OF THIS BOOK

This book focuses on parametric reform of Social Security, but it also discusses issues related to some paradigmatic reform options that have received attention from policy analysts. Paradigmatic reform generally would involve a move toward individual accounts and away from the risk sharing provided by the current Social Security program. Individual accounts have been discussed by Turner (2006), as well as a number of authors. Such a move is already occurring through the decline in employer-provided defined benefit plans and the growth of 401(k) plans and IRAs.

Rather than cover the full range of possible reforms, this book analyzes a set of promising reforms related to increased life expectancy, the increasingly strong relationship between income and life expectancy, the decline in the physical demands of jobs, the rise in income inequality, the pattern of poverty increasing at older ages, and other demographic and economic changes. It also discusses possible reforms to assure Social Security's sustainability and to allow it to do a better job of achieving its goals, particularly in regard to the fairness of the benefit structure. Because an increasing ratio of retirees to workers is making it more costly to provide benefits, future reforms are needed. That ratio is described later as the "price" for current Social Security benefits in a pay-as-you-go system (Turner 1984) and is a key factor in the analysis of Social Security reform, though other issues relating to the distribution of Social Security benefits across different economic and demographic groups also warrant our attention.

Policy analysts sometimes argue that focusing on Social Security reform is too narrow and that the focus should also include other issues such as private pensions, disability, poverty programs, work opportunities for older persons, and health care. While that argument has merit, I do not take that approach here, primarily for reasons of scope. A fuller discussion of issues related to longevity policy (which is policy dealing with retirement and income issues for older Americans resulting from lengthening life spans) can be found in Turner (2011).

This chapter briefly discusses the motivation for the book, given that there are already many books about Social Security. It then discusses the early history and the basics of Social Security—its benefits, its financing, and the need for reform to maintain solvency. The chapter then provides an overview of the remaining chapters.

STAND ON THE SHOULDERS OF GIANTS

A number of excellent books that deal with Social Security reform have already been written. Barr (1993) and Thompson (1998) discuss the economic effects of social security on labor markets, savings, investment, and economic growth; Schieber and Shoven (1999) and Holzmann and Stiglitz (2001) focus in part on the question of adding individual accounts to a Social Security system; Diamond and Orszag (2004) present what they consider to be a balanced approach to Social Security reform; Schieber (2012) discusses whether the Social Security trust funds add to national savings; and Weller (2016) focuses on benefit enhancements for vulnerable groups. In addition, I have written or edited four books covering different aspects of Social Security reform. Gillion et al. (2000) and Szczepański and Turner (2014a) analyze Social Security reform in an international context; Turner (2006) analyzes individual accounts as an aspect of Social Security reform; and Turner (2011) proposes that Social Security adopt an explicit longevity policy, an issue also taken up in this book.

The existence of all this literature prompts the question, why do we need another book on Social Security reform? First, economic analysis has progressed, particularly with the development of behavioral economics, but also with the development of the economics of financial literacy and the economics of financial advice. In addition, researchers continue to study aspects of Social Security and retirement using traditional approaches. Second, the relationship between income and mortality has changed—higher-income people are living substantially longer than lower-income people. Third, the percentage of income above the taxable maximum income has increased substantially. These three developments all suggest the need for changes in the current Social Security system.

This book makes the following contributions: 1) it stresses the role of the old-age dependency ratio as a shadow price for Social Security benefits and how its increase affects Social Security reform, 2) it identifies the exact nature of a sustainable benefit formula, 3) it makes use of recent developments in behavioral economics to propose an improvement of the reform process, and 4) it identifies the role of longevity insurance benefits in the early history of Social Security and proposes that they be restored. In addition, the book argues for an explicit longevity policy for Social Security, as done earlier in Turner (2011).

One of the issues in writing this book was determining the criteria for promising Social Security reforms. An academic reviewer criticized the book for its policy proposals' lacking novelty. Strictly speaking, that is not true since several of the proposals are new. However, most of the proposals discussed in this book have been made earlier, some of them by me. While novelty may be the appropriate criterion for an academic publication, it is a weak criterion for public policy, which should consider proposals that protect vulnerable groups, treat different groups equitably, and are cost effective. Rather than include every proposal that has been scored by the Social Security Actuaries, this book discusses some of the proposals currently debated by presidential candidates for the 2016 election, using that as a filter to determine proposals that are viewed in the political arena as having merit. These proposals are included not for their popularity, which is fleeting as candidates depart from the spotlight. While academics may judge proposals based on their novelty, politicians promote proposals in an attempt to garner votes. Because the cost of the proposals is not always taken into account, this is not a perfect criterion either, but it is at least a real-world test of what politicians think appeals to their constituencies.

HISTORY

Individualism versus Solidarity

Individualism plays a stronger role in American culture than it does in other countries, particularly in Western Europe. With this view, individuals and their families are self-reliant and do not depend on government programs. Through hard work, they are able to meet their own needs. Another vision of society that is more common in some European countries is solidarity, in which people recognize that capitalism can have losers as well as winners, and sometimes things occur through no fault of individuals that make it difficult for them to meet their needs through the market economy.

These two views of society lead to two different views of retirement programs. With the individualistic view, individuals and families save for retirement primarily on their own or through their employers. With solidarity, government social security programs are needed to assure that all individuals have adequate resources in retirement.

Social Security was enacted during the Great Depression, which demonstrated forcefully that individuals are not always able to rely on their own efforts in labor markets to support themselves and their families. It gave support to a movement in society favoring government programs based on solidarity, which collectively are sometimes called the New Deal programs.

The politics of support for Social Security has changed over time. Arguably, the increase in support for an individualistic form of retirement savings, such as individual savings accounts, occurred during the long bull market for stocks leading up to the election of President George W. Bush. That support was due in part to the passage of time since a major event had pointed out the shortcomings of relying primarily on the financial market for providing retirement income. It also may be attributed to changing demographics, with an aging population raising the old-age dependency ratio and making it more costly to provide benefits. The language used to describe Social Security as an entitlement program (rather than as a risk sharing or social insurance program) has negative connotations for those who favor an individualistic approach to providing retirement income, such as those supporting President George W. Bush's proposal for individual accounts. Turmoil in the stock market since 2000 presumably has eroded support for individual accounts because it has underscored the financial risks involved with that approach.

Longevity Insurance Benefits

While some fundamental aspects of Social Security have not changed since its inception in 1940 when Social Security began providing benefits, it was a much different program than it is currently in terms of the nature of the benefits it provided. The benefit eligibility age was set at 65 for two reasons: 1) pension plans at that time generally used either age 65 or 70 as the eligibility age, and 2) actuarial calculations indicated that sufficiently few people would qualify at age 65 that the program could be financed with a low payroll tax rate (Social Security Administration 2016a). Life expectancy at age 65 was 11.9 years (Bell and Miller 2005). Taking into account the fact that people entered the workforce at earlier ages than they do now, 54 percent of that population would still be alive at age 65 (Glover 1921). Thus, Social Security provided benefits at a relatively advanced age at which roughly half of those entering the workforce in their youth had died, and the benefits were not provided for much more than a decade of retirement on average.

Over time, three changes have fundamentally altered the nature of the old-age benefits that Social Security provides: 1) the benefit eligibility age was lowered to age 62, 2) life expectancy has increased, and 3) people enter the workforce at older ages. Whereas earlier, barely half of workforce entrants survived to receive Social Security benefits, now 88 percent of 20-year-olds survive to age 62 to be eligible to receive Social Security benefits (Arias 2014). By comparison, had the retirement age remained at 65 and the workforce entry age remained at 18, 81 percent of 18-year-olds would still be alive at age 65, compared to 54 percent in 1940. Therefore, most of the increase in the likelihood of surviving to receive benefits is due to improvements in life expectancy rather than the reduction in the benefit eligibility age or later entry into the workforce.

For the population aged 20 in 2008, 50 percent would still be alive at age 82 (Arias 2014). Thus, translating the original Social Security program into the current setting, according to this measure, Social Security would be a program that started paying benefits at age 82.

Using twenty-first century terminology, Social Security at its start could be characterized as a longevity insurance benefit program. Longevity insurance benefits are provided at an old age, when roughly half of those entering the workforce will have died, thus making them relatively low-cost benefits. Social Security was originally structured as a low-cost longevity insurance program providing benefits at an advanced age to roughly half of the people who entered the workforce. Largely due to improvements in life expectancy, it has transformed into a more costly, broad-based program providing old-age benefits for most of the population that entered the workforce in their youth.

Costs

In 2010, life expectancy at age 62 was 23.3 years (Bell and Miller 2005), compared to 11.9 years at age 65 in 1940. The doubling of life expectancy at the benefit eligibility age roughly doubles the cost of providing Social Security benefits. These two factors combined—the increase in survivorship to receive benefits and the doubling of life expectancy at the benefit eligibility age—account for a substantial part of the cost increase.

Projecting into the future, because of the aging U.S. population, the percentage of gross domestic product that will be spent on providing Social Security benefits will rise from almost 5 percent in 2014 to 6 percent in 2039. While this is not a large change, dealing with it is made more difficult by larger increases in other federal government benefit programs for health care for older persons. Those expenditures will grow by three times as much, from just under 5 percent of GDP in 2014 to 8 percent of GDP in 2039 (Niu and Topoleski 2014).

THE BASICS OF SOCIAL SECURITY

Despite the current large size of its trust fund, over the long term Social Security is designed to be financed on a pay-as-you-go basis, meaning that annual benefit payments roughly equal annual payroll tax receipts. It is not funded like a private sector pension plan, which must have advance funding roughly equal to its liabilities for future benefit payments. It has an unfunded liability that is not counted as part of the national debt of the United States. Social Security is not financed by general tax revenues and is thus not a liability against them in the future; rather, it is financed by the payroll tax.

Benefits

Social Security provides benefits based on a formula and thus differs from defined contribution plans, such as 401(k) plans, where benefits are based on the amount saved in an individual account. Workers must pay Social Security taxes or contributions for 10 years to be eligible for benefits. Social Security pools economic risks that individuals face, such as unemployment and wage growth risks, as well as demographic risks, such as the risk of outliving one's income by living longer than expected.

Social Security provides benefits in the form of a price-indexed annuity. It provides monthly benefits that continue until the worker's death and then provides survivor benefits to the worker's spouse if the spouse qualifies for those benefits. It provides a base level of benefits, with most workers needing to supplement it with pensions and savings. Social Security, pensions, and savings are often referred to as the "three-legged stool" of retirement income, though many people do not have a pension or substantial savings. Some retirees, particularly those in their sixties, supplement Social Security benefits with earnings from work.

Social Security calculates individual benefits based on the average of the worker's 35 highest years of wage-indexed earnings. For workers with less than 35 years of earnings, zeroes are added in for the missing years when calculating average earnings. The worker's total indexed monthly earnings in the high 35 years are divided by the product of 35 × 12 to determine the average indexed monthly earnings (AIME).

An alternative approach that would have the advantage of including all covered earnings would be to base benefits on total lifetime indexed covered earnings rather than average earnings. That approach would thus count all covered earnings and could have the effect of encouraging (rather than discouraging) continued work at older ages.

The formula for estimating an individual and spouse's Social Security benefits is complex. It can be thought of as occurring in four steps: 1) calculate the AIMEs, 2) calculate the worker's primary insurance amount (PIA), 3) make adjustments for early or late retirement, and 4) calculate the spouse or survivor benefits. These four steps are explained more fully below.

First, benefits are computed based on career wages, but only on wages up to the taxable maximum. The taxable maximum earnings rises in line with wage inflation. Wages in earlier years also are indexed in the benefit calculation. In the United States, rather than indexing these wages for price inflation, they are indexed based on the growth in economy-wide average wages.

Wages are indexed up to the year the worker turns 60. Wages earned after age 60 are included without deflating them back to the base earnings as of age 60 (expressing them in age-60 earnings, which would be lower because of the effect of inflation over time).

Second, workers retiring at the normal retirement age receive a benefit called the PIA. For many years, the normal retirement age, which refers to a parameter in the benefit formula and not to when most people retire, was age 65. It is now slowly increasing to age 67. For persons reaching age 62 before 2000, the normal retirement age was 65. It will increase gradually to 67 for persons reaching that age in 2027 or later.

The PIA is calculated from the AIME using a benefit formula that has three segments. At the end of the first earnings segment, AIMEs—which in 2016 are up to $856—are multiplied by 0.9. AIMEs in the second earnings segment, between $856 and $5,157, are multiplied by 0.32. AIMEs in the third earnings segment, above $5,157, are multiplied by 0.15. Then the three amounts are combined to determine the PIA. The maximum earnings for each segment are called the bend points of the Social Security benefit formula because when the formula is graphed, they are points where the slope of the line indicating the relationship between the AIME and the PIA changes. Possible changes in the Social Security benefit formula are discussed in Chapter 3.

Third, benefits first received at ages other than the normal retirement age are increased or decreased for later or earlier retirement. Fourth, as well as providing benefits to workers based on their labor market earnings, the program also provides benefits to spouses of workers who have not worked or who have fewer years of work or lower earnings than their higher-earning spouses. Social Security also provides survivor benefits to those spouses upon the death of the insured worker. A person can receive spouse and survivor benefits if those are higher than the person's own retired worker benefits. A spouse cannot claim a spouse benefit until the other spouse claims his or her retired worker's benefit.

Survivor benefits can be claimed beginning at age 60, but spousal benefits cannot be claimed until age 62. The spousal benefit depends on the age at which the spouse retires. If the person receiving the spousal benefits claims those benefits between age 62 and their full retirement age, the amount will be permanently reduced by a percentage based on the number of months up to his or her full retirement age. If the person receiving spousal benefits starts taking those benefits at his or her full retirement age, the benefits will be half as much as the worker's benefits. The exact determination of survivor benefits is complicated (Henriques 2012), but survivor benefits are affected by the age at which the spouse claims benefits because delayed claiming, up to age 70, raises the worker's benefit. The survivor's benefit equals the worker's benefit.

The benefit formula with its lower adjustment factor for higher earners is progressive, meaning that it provides more generous benefits relative to past earnings for those who have lower earnings. The progressivity in annual benefits is offset somewhat, however, when considering lifetime benefits, because people with higher earnings tend to live longer than people with lower earnings. The progressivity is also offset because people with higher earnings tend to postpone receipt of Social Security benefits, which currently they can do on a favorable basis. The lifetime value of Social Security benefits goes up for most workers postponing their receipt (up to age 70), even if the person does not continue working, but the gain from postponing is greater for people with longer life expectancy, who tend to be people with higher incomes.

In 2013, the average annual benefit for a worker and spouse was $24,660 and for a widow or widower was $14,604 (Reno and Walker 2013). Social Security benefits in payment are adjusted each year that there is price inflation to keep up with the Consumer Price Index for Urban Wage Earners and Clerical Workers (CPI-W). Upper-income beneficiaries pay income taxes on part of their Social Security benefits, but for the rest of recipients the benefits are received tax free.

To help participants plan for their future Social Security benefits, the Social Security Administration announced in 2014 that it would send Social Security Statements once every five years for most people—for those aged 25, 30, 35, 40, 45, 50, 55, and 60—and every year for people aged 61 and older who are not already receiving benefits (Social Security Administration 2014). Because the growth of 401(k) plans is placing greater responsibility on workers for retirement planning, it is important that the government provides reliable information about future Social Security benefits and possible changes in those benefits (Kritzer and Smith 2016). However, the usefulness of these statements for younger workers is questionable because these benefit statements assume that promised Social Security benefits will be paid. It is likely, especially for younger workers, that Social Security reform will result in less generous benefits than promised in current law, which raises the point that the uncertain future of Social Security, with its future insolvency, creates a problem for financial planning for retirement and financial advice relating to retirement.

Also in 2014, Social Security began providing benefits to same-sex couples who were legally married or who were in a nonmarital relationship that could be considered marriage for the purposes of claiming Social Security benefits. This change was the result of the Supreme Court case *United States vs. Windsor*, which found part of the Defense of Marriage Act to be unconstitutional.

While most people think of Social Security benefits as annual benefit amounts received, economists use the concept of Social Security wealth to measure the lifetime value of Social Security benefits. Social Security wealth is the expected present value of Social Security benefits. This wealth concept, however, understates the utility value of Social Security benefits to participants because it does not include the value of the insurance Social Security provides as an annuity, wherein it provides benefits as long as the person is alive, which provides insurance against outliving one's income. Social Security wealth also does not take into account the utility value of Social Security providing benefits that are price indexed, thus protecting the recipient against the effects of inflation.

Financing

Most workers in the United States pay the Social Security payroll tax to finance the benefits the program provides. About a quarter of state and local government workers do not participate in Social Security (Reno and John 2012).

Because Social Security benefits and Social Security taxes are both based on the worker's earnings, the Social Security tax differs from other taxes in that there is a direct link through the benefit formula between taxes paid and benefits received (Burkhauser and Turner 1985). For those who ultimately receive Social Security benefits based on their own earnings, increases in earnings, up to the Social Security taxable maximum earnings, raise future benefits. It is not clear whether workers perceive the details of this relationship, but it appears likely that they do understand the relatively simple concept that increases in their earnings lead to increases in future Social Security benefits. The generosity of the link between taxes and benefits varies across the population because of the progressive nature of the benefit formula and other factors, but if an individual pays more Social Security payroll taxes, she generally receives more in future benefits. Because of the connection between taxes paid and benefits received, the Social Security payroll tax arguably does not have some of the adverse effects that other taxes have, such as affecting decisions about work, or at least to the same extent (Burkhauser and Turner 1985).

The Social Security payroll tax is officially called the Federal Insurance Contributions Act (FICA) tax; half is paid by workers and half is paid by their employers. The half paid by workers is not deducted from their taxable incomes, and thus they pay federal income tax on that money. The half paid by employers is not added to their taxable incomes, and thus they do not pay income tax on that money. Since employers do not give away money, economists generally argue that the employer half of the payroll tax is ultimately borne by workers through reduced wages. The amount paid by the employer is deductible by the employer as a business expense. Self-employed workers pay both the employee and employer share of the payroll tax, but only half of the tax amount is treated as taxable income. Therefore, self-employed workers can deduct half of their Social Security payroll tax payments from their taxable incomes.

The OASI payroll tax rate in 2015 was 10.6 percent (employer and employee share), and the Bipartisan Budget Act of 2015 temporarily reallocated a portion of it to the Disability Insurance program for 2016–2018. Beginning in 2019, the tax rate for OASI will revert to its 2015 rate. The payroll tax rate is set by law, and no future increases in the payroll tax rate are legislated. It is levied on the worker's earnings up to a taxable maximum, which was $118,500 in 2016—about 6 percent of workers have earnings above that amount. The maximum is indexed for changes in the national average wage index and is adjusted annually.

The money collected through the Social Security tax is paid into a Social Security Trust Fund, where it is used to buy government bonds. The interest on these bonds is credited to the trust fund, which is used to pay benefits and administrative expenses (Reno and Walker 2013).

OVERVIEW OF THE BOOK

This book discusses four policy goals for Social Security: 1) achieving fiscal sustainability, 2) balancing the trade-off between system affordability and benefit adequacy, 3) improving equity in the distribution of benefits across different types of workers and retirees, and 4) reducing political risk. Some of these goals overlap, and some involve trade-offs against other goals.

While the book focuses on benefit adequacy, particularly for lower-income workers, and financial sustainability as the most important issues in reform, Chapter 2 also discusses other criteria that have been proposed for evaluating Social Security reform, including equity and labor market efficiency. Trade-offs occur between benefit adequacy for lower-income workers and equity, which is taken to mean an equal rate of return on contributions for workers in different income groups.

Chapter 2 explains why the Social Security system is no longer sustainable under its current benefit formula in the face of population aging. It discusses the basic options for assuring solvency—raising revenues, cutting benefits, and raising the early retirement age (while adjusting the calculation of benefits so that benefits received at age 62 would be instead received at age 63). It considers the possibility of investing part of the Social Security trust fund in the stock market. It discusses the constraints that exist if policymakers decide, for example, that the payroll tax cannot be raised, or that benefits cannot be cut. While adequacy and sustainability involve trade-offs, reforms that are fiscally sustainable may not be politically sustainable if they involve declining replacement rates over time. Thus, the book examines both fiscal and political sustainability in terms of preserving adequate replacement rates.

Chapter 3 examines Social Security benefits and the difficulties in defining their adequacy and offers alternate definitions. While the preceding chapter looks at adequacy as part of a macro level reform, this chapter discusses achieving adequacy through better targeting of Social Security benefits. It considers changes in Social Security benefits that could be made in recognition of longer life expectancy, such as the possible role of longevity insurance benefits beginning at age 82. That discussion takes into account the implications of the cross-sectional pattern of changes in life expectancy in the United States, where the improvements have been much greater for upper-income workers than for lower-income workers. This chapter includes a discussion of using the chained CPI to index Social Security benefits in payment, noting that it may be a more accurate measure of inflation, but that it has adverse consequences as a benefits policy because it cuts benefits most for the oldest recipients.

Chapter 4 discusses retirement issues, such as when to take Social Security benefits, and notes various strategies for taking benefits. It also discusses reforms that would affect when people retire, such as raising the early retirement age.

Chapter 5 examines issues in the democratic process of Social Security reform and considers behavioral aspects of public policy-making that make it difficult in the United States to achieve Social Security reform. The use of a 75-year horizon for benefit solvency may increase the difficulty of reform because it marks as inadequate reforms that assure solvency for a shorter period. It discusses automatic adjustment mechanisms that some countries have adopted to deal with these issues.

Chapter 6 summarizes the book and provides a set of reform recommendations.

A BALANCED APPROACH

Social Security reform is a controversial topic, with people holding markedly different views as to how it should be accomplished. Recognizing that policy analysts disagree as to what constitutes a balanced analysis, this book nonetheless attempts to provide such a review and at the same time assess what the best approaches may be. While an approach that takes a clearly liberal or conservative perspective would probably please roughly half of Social Security policy experts, a balanced approach does not have a clearly identifiable group of supporters. Recognizing that dilemma, to successfully reform Social Security, a spirit of compromise in policymaking will be needed.

Note

1. I follow the convention that references to the Social Security program in the United States are capitalized, while references to social security programs in other countries or to social security as a concept are not capitalized.

Chapter 2

Sustainability and Financing Reform

Social Security is not financially sustainable with its current benefit formula, which promises more benefits than the financing can support. Reform that either cuts benefits or raises taxes or both will be required. The *2015 Social Security Trustees' Report* (2015) projects that there will be insufficient assets in the OASI trust fund in 2035, less than 20 years away. At that point, Social Security will have sufficient income to pay 77 percent of scheduled benefits. The Congressional Budget Office (2015b) projects that insolvency will occur in 2031, in part because it projects greater increases in life expectancy than does the Social Security Administration.

In 1994, Steuerle and Bakija (p. 3) wrote, "That future reform is inevitable, and not simply a political intention, is crucial for policymakers and the American public to comprehend." Two decades later the statement is still true, but Social Security reform has not yet occurred.

The options for achieving financial sustainability now, as they were two decades ago, are limited to increasing revenues, reducing benefits, and raising retirement ages (with the benefits paid at the earlier age being paid at the new retirement age). Looking to international experience, Canada has achieved sustainability primarily by raising revenue, while Germany has achieved sustainability primarily by cutting benefits. In its major reform, Sweden raised the retirement age, among other changes (Turner and Rajnes 2016).

This chapter explains why the Social Security system was sustainable earlier in its history but is not sustainable under its current benefit formula in the face of population aging. It discusses the basic options for restoring and assuring solvency and considers one reform that could be considered a paradigmatic reform—investing part of the Social Security trust fund in the stock market. Canada has successfully implemented such a reform. The chapter considers the constraints that exist if policymakers decide that the payroll tax cannot be raised further or benefits cannot be cut. While adequacy and sustainability involve trade-offs, reforms that are fiscally sustainable may not be politically sustainable if they involve declining replacement rates over time. Thus, the chapter examines both fiscal sustainability and political sustainability in terms of preserving adequate replacement rates.

RAISING REVENUE

Raising the Payroll Tax Rate

Raising the Social Security payroll tax rate is one way to achieve financial sustainability for Social Security. From 1980 to 1990, the rate increased by a total of 2.24 percentage points. The highest increase in one year was 0.72 percentage points, which was the increase in the combined employee and employer parts of the payroll tax. In 2011 and 2012, the employee portion of the payroll tax was temporarily cut by 2 percentage points as an economic stimulus to encourage employment, but then in 2013 the cut was ended, so the payroll tax rate rose that year by 2 percentage points.

In a 2013 Google Consumer Survey, the Center for Economic and Policy Research asked people whether the Social Security tax had been raised, lowered, or left the same at the beginning of the year. Most answered that they didn't know, while 29 percent correctly answered that the tax had gone up. To test the hypothesis that some people would always answer that the Social Security payroll tax rate had increased because they think that the government is raising taxes, the same question was asked in 2014, when no change had occurred. In that year, 20 percent answered incorrectly that it had gone up. Comparing these two results, it can be argued that only 9 percent actually noticed the increase in 2013, with 20 percent in any year saying that it had increased (Baker and Woo 2014). Based on this result, it appears that most people do not perceive a small increase in the Social Security payroll tax rate as part of a reform package as having a negative effect.

Baker and Woo (2014) argue that an important reason why few people noticed the increase in the payroll tax was that both political parties agreed that it should occur. Thus, there was no political contentiousness drawing attention to it and bashing the president or the party in power. Consequently, the press did not focus on it as a partisan issue. Had one political party strongly opposed the increase, the survey results would probably have shown much greater awareness of the increase. Thus, the acceptability of the payroll tax rate increase to the public arguably was due to its bipartisan acceptance in Congress.

Raising the Taxable Maximum Earnings

Another option to raise revenue would be to increase the percentage of labor earnings in the economy that is subject to the payroll tax. That would be achieved by raising the taxable maximum earnings level. About 7 percent of workers earn more than the taxable maximum. In 1937, when Social Security payroll taxes were first collected, about 92 percent of earnings of workers covered by Social Security was below the taxable maximum (Congressional Budget Office 2015b). Over time, the percentage of labor earnings subject to the payroll tax has fallen because of the relatively faster growth of income above the Social Security taxable maximum income level than below it. In 2015, about 81 percent of the earning of workers covered by Social Security was under the taxable maximum earnings (Congressional Budget Office 2015b).

Raising the taxable maximum from its 2016 level of $118,500 to $255,000 would eliminate about a quarter of Social Security's 75-year deficit. It would allow Social Security to tax the same share of earnings that it did in the 1980s, before the surge in income for high-earners reduced the percentage of earnings that was taxable under the Social Security payroll tax (Peterson 2015).

"Soaking the Rich"

Since its inception, Social Security financing has taken into account equity, in that participants receive a benefit that is tied to their contributions. However, an alternative policy, which can be categorized as "doing good with other people's money" (or "soaking the rich"), is greatly raising or eliminating the cap on taxable earnings and also taxing non–labor market income for higher-income persons. Because Social Security benefits are based on taxable labor market earnings, this change would also raise benefits for high-income workers. To deal with this issue, a cap could be placed on earnings used for the purpose of calculating benefits but not for the purpose of payroll tax payments. Another alternative would be to raise the cap on taxable earnings for workers but eliminate it for employers. Thus, employers would pay their half of the payroll tax for persons earning, for example, more than a million dollars a year, but benefits for those persons would be based on the taxable ceiling for their share of the payroll tax. However, from an economics perspective, it is assumed that workers ultimately bear the payroll tax rate paid by employers through employers reducing their wages below what they otherwise would be, so high earners presumably would effectively bear the employer's payroll tax payments. The United Kingdom has eliminated the ceiling for the employer contribution. In addition, it has eliminated the ceiling for employee contributions, but employees contribute above the ceiling at a reduced rate of 2 percent of pay.

Other Sources of Revenue

Social Security has been financed almost entirely (96 percent) by the payroll tax, and partially (4 percent) by the income tax on Social Security benefits of retirees with higher incomes (Congressional Budget Office 2015b). Some people, however, have proposed supplementing that funding with general revenue funding, which presumably would be more progressive, meaning that a relatively smaller portion of the burden would be placed on low-income workers because the Social Security payroll tax is not levied on income above the taxable maximum earnings. Thus, people with high incomes do not pay the Social Security payroll tax on their labor earnings above that amount. Canada, Australia, and Japan all use general revenue funding to differing degrees, and that source of funding appears to work well in those countries.

Several arguments have been made against using general revenue funding to finance Social Security. As Schieber (2012) notes, President Franklin D. Roosevelt opposed it because he believed that a program fully funded that way would be viewed as a welfare program and would not have as much political support. Some argue that having dedicated funding for Social Security provides fiscal discipline for the program because it forces the program to keep within a set budget. However, dedicated funding provides political protection for Social Security, in that people feel like they have paid for their benefits, making it more difficult to cut them. In the countries that use general revenue funding, these arguments against its use do not seem to have merit, though they could still apply within the U.S. political system.

Altman (2015) argues that the estate tax is a legacy tax that could be used to help pay off the legacy costs of Social Security. The logic of the argument is that Social Security has incurred legacy costs because the first generation of benefit recipients, who had suffered the economic catastrophe of the Great Depression, received far more in benefits than they had paid for. This intergenerational transfer from later, higher-income generations to the first generation can be justified based on the economic hardship that generation suffered.

Other sources of revenue could also be used. For example, unclaimed pension benefits in defined contribution plans, assets that have benefited from favorable tax treatment for the purposes of providing retirement income, could be used for Social Security financing

(Bruce and Turner 2003). With defined benefit plans, if the benefit is unclaimed the money stays in the plan, ultimately to the benefit of the plan sponsor who needs to contribute less to fund promised benefits. The money is owned not by the plan or plan sponsor but by the individual participant. Nonetheless, for various reasons, such as workers forgetting about or not being able to find pensions at previous jobs, some defined contribution accounts are never claimed. Using this unclaimed money for Social Security financing would solve the problem of what to do with it, and it would have the advantage of keeping the money within the retirement income system.

Extending Coverage to State and Local Government Workers

About 25 percent of state and local government workers—6.5 million workers—are not covered by Social Security. A proposal to cover all newly hired state and local government workers would finance about 8 percent of Social Security's funding gap (Reno and John 2012). Diamond and Orszag (2004) argue that Social Security coverage should be extended to all state and local government workers. When Social Security was first established, large transfers were made to the initial generation of beneficiaries, who had suffered economically during the Great Depression and World War II. Diamond and Orszag (2004) argue that the cost of those transfers should be borne by all contemporary workers, including the relatively well-paid workers in state and local governments who currently do not participate in Social Security.

Investing in the Stock Market

One way to raise revenues is to invest part of the Social Security trust fund in the stock market. Countries establish trust funds for their pay-as-you-go social security programs in order to smooth out variations in contributions that occur over time, in part due to changes in the unemployment rate. A few countries have invested some of the assets of their social security trust fund in financial markets to improve expected returns and diversify risks.

This policy can be viewed as a form of social security privatization, in that the assets held by the social security program are invested in the private sector. It increases the financial risks associated with the trust fund investments compared to the current approach, but the greater risk of well-diversified investments is compensated for by greater expected reward. A diversified portfolio of stocks and bonds, combined with a strategy of asset rebalancing to control risk, would reduce financial market risk and generally earn a higher rate of return than does the current trust fund investment in government bonds. Investing in the stock market this way would involve substantially lower administrative costs than individual accounts, and investment and mortality risks would be pooled more effectively (Munnell and Sass 2006).

The Canada Pension Plan (CPP) invests its trust fund assets in financial markets, and the investments are managed by the CPP Investment Board (CPPIB), a professional investment management organization that is independent of political influence (CPPIB 2013a).[1] Canada has achieved independence from political influence through the governance structure of the CPPIB, which is accountable to an independent board of directors.

The Canada Pension Plan invests in a wide range of assets—in 2013, 50.0 percent of its investments were in equities, 33.1 percent were in fixed income, and 16.9 percent were in real assets, including real estate (CPPIB 2013b). The investments include public equities, private equities, corporate and government bonds, private debt, infrastructure, real estate, and other investments. In fiscal year 2015, the CPP earned a net rate of return (after fees) of 18.5 percent. Its annualized 5- and 10-year rates of return were 12.3 percent and 8.0 percent, respectively (CPPIB 2016). By comparison, in 2014, the OASI trust fund earned a rate of return of 3.6 percent on the government bonds that it holds (Social Security Administration 2016b). If the trust fund earned a higher rate of return, that would help reduce Social Security's future deficit.

The Thrift Savings Plan for most U.S. federal government workers is the largest defined contribution plan in the United States and provides a model for how government-managed investing can be done without political interference. It is entirely passively managed, with all its investments in index funds. The CPP investments, by contrast, are actively managed.

A funded system can be invested in government bonds, as is currently done for the Social Security trust funds, or it can be partially or fully invested in financial markets. An unfunded social security system involves implicit future liabilities for the government, while a system invested in government bonds involves explicit liabilities for the government. In that sense, assuming the government has equal responsibility for paying promised benefits in both cases, there is little difference between the two approaches. However, investing in equities would be substantially different in its risk characteristics from having an unfunded system.

Munnell (2013) argues in favor of investing part of the trust funds in the stock market. She argues that doing so would make it more difficult to use the trust funds to cover shortfalls in other parts of the government budget. With current government accounting, if Social Security has a surplus of $100 billion and the rest of the budget has a deficit of $150 billion, on net the government has a deficit of $50 billion. If, however, the trust funds had invested the $100 billion in the stock market, that would be considered an outlay, and the government budget deficit would be measured as $150 billion, which provides a more accurate accounting of government finances.

An argument against investing the Social Security trust funds in the stock market is that a pay-as-you-go system is subject to risks that differ from financial market risks. Thus, maintaining a pay-as-you-go system alongside a private pension system and private savings is a way of diversifying risks in a broad social policy sense.

CUTTING BENEFITS

While a balanced approach to restoring solvency would seem to involve both benefit cuts and revenue increases, some argue that benefit cuts for low-income seniors would be unconscionable because, by international standards, the level of U.S. Social Security benefits is already quite low. Generally, proposals for cutting benefits are targeted at future retirees and leave the benefits of current retirees untouched. This approach is generally favored because many current retirees have no way to offset the benefit cuts. Some future retirees could extend their working lives to offset the cuts or they could save more on their own. However, counter to the general principle of not cutting benefits for people already retired, President Obama proposed changes in price indexing that would reduce future benefits of current retirees.

Many people, particularly at older ages, rely almost exclusively on Social Security for their retirement income, and because of that their retirement incomes are quite low. Cutting benefits for those people would cause real harm. For this reason, it would appear that benefit cuts should not be across-the-board cuts but instead should be targeted, such as by excluding people aged 80 and older. This type of targeting is functionally similar to providing a longevity insurance benefit at age 80, which is a proposal discussed in Chapter 3.

Raising the early retirement age in Social Security (62) so that benefits can be received at age 63 is yet another step that can be taken to restore solvency to Social Security. This option is discussed in Chapter 4. We note here, however, that the policy discussed is not an immediate raising of the early retirement age but, rather, an increase that would occur with a delay and would then be phased in. Proposals to immediately raise the early retirement age would be unfair to people near retirement who had made their plans based on knowing that they would be able to claim Social Security benefits at age 62.

INDIVIDUAL ACCOUNTS AND FUNDING

Funded individual accounts are like 401(k) pension accounts, which are the most common type of employer-provided defined contribution plan in the United States. Each individual has his or her own account to which money is contributed and invested. Funded individual accounts have been used to partially or fully replace traditional pay-as-you-go social security programs in Chile and in some other countries, primarily in South America and in Central and Eastern Europe. With funded individual accounts, the ultimate benefit depends on the amount contributed to the account by the worker, and possibly the employer and the government, the rates of return received, and the fees charged against the accounts.

A fundamental problem with this type of reform involving social security privatization is known as "paying twice." While workers are paying into the new funded accounts, they must continue paying for the benefits already promised in the pay-as-you-go system. Some countries transitioning from communist economies have been able to deal with the paying twice problem to some extent by using the proceeds of sales from state-owned enterprises to help pay for the benefits in the pay-as-you-go system. Obviously, that approach is not an option in the United States, and the paying twice problem is a major obstacle to Social Security reform involving individual accounts in the United States.

If the goal of reform is funding or partial funding, that does not require individual accounts. Funding can occur within the current Social Security program. Canada's partially funded social security program provides an example of a successful reform of this type. With its partial funding, the system is projected to maintain solvency over the next 75 years with no future increases in payroll taxes or cuts in benefits. From the U.S. perspective, that is a remarkable achievement.

With either funded individual accounts or a partially funded traditional Social Security system, the issue of investment risk arises.

Investing the assets in financial markets results in investment risk. (See Samborski and Turner [2015] for a discussion of different kinds of risk.) That is of course true for any investment, including any pension investment, and it may be that the higher expected rate of return justifies the added risk.

A SUSTAINABLE SOCIAL SECURITY BENEFIT FORMULA

It is commonly argued that Social Security is not sustainable because of demographic changes—the combination of people living longer and fewer births. This chapter contends that the reason is not demography but rather a flaw in the Social Security benefit formula that causes the system to be unsustainable in the face of these demographic changes.

This section analyzes the characteristics of a sustainable Social Security benefit formula in a pay-as-you-go system. Some people argue that the payroll tax rate should not be raised further. Such a policy has consequences for the generosity of Social Security benefits. Appendix 2A, the mathematical appendix to this chapter, indicates that a consequence of not raising the payroll tax rate would be that a sustainable Social Security program would have benefits growing at the rate of real wage growth less an adjustment for the rate of growth in the old-age dependency ratio, which is the ratio of Social Security beneficiaries to covered workers. Many countries, including the United States, are seeking to maintain the generosity of their social security benefits. The current demographics of an increasing old-age dependency ratio, if combined with a fixed payroll tax rate, dictate that the Social Security replacement rate must fall. It is not possible to maintain the current generosity of Social Security with an increasing old-age dependency ratio and a fixed payroll tax rate. This conclusion derives from the pay-as-you-go budget constraint, which is that current tax payments must be sufficient to pay for current benefits. The dynamic pay-as-you-go budget constraint is that the growth in tax payments must be sufficient to pay for the growth in benefits. With the labor force growing slower than the number of beneficiaries and the payroll tax rate fixed, the growth rate in real benefits must be less than the growth rate in real wages for a pay-as-you-go system to maintain its financial balance.

The social security budget constraint limits countries' social security options. If countries have decided that they will not raise the social security payroll tax rate or will not reduce benefits, their choices are further limited. Because of relatively low birth rates and increasing life expectancy at older ages, the number of beneficiaries is growing faster than the number of workers.

POLITICAL SUSTAINABILITY

A social security benefit formula or automatic adjustment formula that is financially sustainable may not be politically sustainable. In particular, the replacement ratio or benefit generosity level may eventually cause benefits to fall to a level of generosity that is not politically acceptable. Some people already believe that that point has been reached. Further adjustments may be needed to maintain the generosity of social security benefits, such as gradually increasing the early retirement age over time. That policy is discussed in more detail in Chapter 3. Such an adjustment may be justified as life expectancy and health at older ages continue to improve, while the percentage of the workforce with physically demanding jobs is declining. Many countries have made this change, which can penalize workers who are no longer able to work, often those at the lower end of the income scale whose jobs are low skilled or involve physical labor. Such an adjustment should take into consideration the needs of workers unable to continue working because of unemployment, the physical nature of their jobs, and their health.

An alternative approach is to provide a flat benefit in addition to the existing earnings-related benefit, which would be funded from general revenue (Lind et al. 2013). This proposal is similar to the approach taken in Canada and Ireland. A variant of this approach that has some appeal is to provide a flat benefit starting at age 82. This is a form of longevity insurance benefits, which start at advanced ages. They are discussed further in Chapter 3.

CONCLUSIONS

The Social Security pay-as-you-go budget constraint can be analyzed to determine the properties of sustainability for social security programs, either through the structure of their benefit formulas or through automatic adjustment mechanisms. While people disagree about the politically acceptable level of the payroll tax rate, when countries reach the point where further increases in the payroll tax rate are no longer politically feasible, the implications for the generosity of social security benefits become clear. With increasing old-age dependency ratios, the generosity of benefits, as measured by the replacement ratio, must decline. This decline can be offset by increasing the age of eligibility for benefits.

This chapter explains the requirements for a benefit formula for pay-as-you-go social security programs that will assure solvency over the long run. The benefit formula automatically adjusts to economic and demographic changes in a way that is stable and sustainable. The United States has a relatively low payroll tax rate for Social Security compared to other countries, and thus presumably has room for further increases. Once a country reaches its maximum acceptable social security payroll tax rate, a social security system with a benefit formula that sets the growth in average real benefits over time equal to the growth in the real wage minus the growth in the old-age dependency ratio will be sustainable with respect to demographic and economic fluctuations. Social security programs, such as that in the United States, that set the rate of growth of real benefits per beneficiary equal to the rate of growth of real wages, which maintains a constant replacement rate over time, will not be sustainable over the long run because of population aging.

Note

1. According to the most recent report by the Chief Actuary of Canada (released November 2013), the CPP is sustainable throughout the report's 75-year projection period. Contributions are projected to exceed annual benefits paid through 2022, after which a portion of the CPPIB investment income will be needed to help pay retirement benefits (Office of the Superintendent of Financial Institutions 2013).

Appendix 2A

Mathematical Derivation of a Sustainable Social Security Benefit Formula

With a pay-as-you-go social security system, the total benefits paid out in a year equal the total payroll tax payments received. That relationship can be expressed in Equation (2A.1) as a budget constraint, where B is average benefits in real terms, N is the total number of beneficiaries, t is the payroll tax rate (or contribution rate), w is the average real wage, and L is the number of workers.

$$(2A.1) \quad BN = twL$$

That budget constraint can be rewritten in terms of percentage changes over time, where E is the percentage change operator (technically, the derivative of the natural logarithm).

$$(2A.2) \quad E(BN) = E(twL)$$

For social security to continue to maintain financial balance, the growth rate in total real benefit payments must equal the growth rate in total real payroll tax payments.

For countries that have a fixed payroll tax rate, t, having reached the maximum level considered politically acceptable, the constraint becomes

$$(2A.3) \quad E(BN) = E(wL)$$

Thus, the growth rate in total real benefit payments must equal the growth rate in total real wages. This constraint can be disaggregated into the growth rates in its component parts and expressed in terms of the economic and demographic changes that limit the sustainable growth in real benefits, and then expressed as a formula for the growth rate in average real benefits per beneficiary.

$$(2A.4) \quad E(B) + E(N) = E(w) + E(L)$$

(2A.5) $E(B) = E(w) + E(L) - E(N)$

Thus, Equation (2A.5) indicates that to maintain solvency, the growth rate in average real benefits must equal the growth rate in real wages plus the difference between the growth rate in the labor force and the growth rate in beneficiaries. In most advanced western countries, because of population aging, the growth rate in beneficiaries exceeds the growth rate of the labor force.

Changes in the ratio of beneficiaries to covered workers (the old-age dependency ratio) play a key role in social security financing in pay-as-you-go systems.

(2A.6) $E(B) = E(w) - E(N/L)$

Equation (2A.6) indicates that a sustainable social security program would have benefits growing at the rate of real wage growth less an adjustment for the rate of growth in the old-age dependency ratio. Equations (2A.5) and (2A.6) are different expressions of the fundamental equation for constructing a sustainable automatic adjustment mechanism or benefit formula. Mechanisms or benefit formulas that are not consistent with those equations will not be sustainable over the long run.

Chapter 3

Benefit Adequacy

This chapter discusses achieving benefit adequacy through better targeting of Social Security benefits. It considers the role of longevity insurance benefits for those aged 82 and older, as well as other changes in Social Security benefits that could be made as part of a longevity policy in recognition of longer life expectancy. That discussion takes into account the implications of the cross-sectional pattern of changes in life expectancy in the United States, where the improvements have been much greater for upper-income workers than for lower-income workers. This chapter also examines the chained Consumer Price Index (CPI), noting that it may be a more accurate measure of inflation, but that it has adverse consequences as a benefits policy because it cuts benefits most for the oldest recipients.

MEASURING BENEFIT ADEQUACY

Social Security plays a key role in providing income to U.S. retirees. Nine out of 10 persons aged 65 and older receive Social Security benefits. In 2013, the average Social Security benefit was $1,294 a month, or $15,528 a year. Among persons aged 65 and older, for 22 percent of married couples and 47 percent of unmarried persons, Social Security benefits constituted 90 percent or more of their retirement income (Social Security Administration 2014). Thus, more than a third of retirees rely almost exclusively on their Social Security benefits. About 65 percent of benefit recipients receive Social Security benefits that account for more than half of their retirement income (Reno and Walker 2013).

Retirement income for purposes of these statistics is measured as regular income receipts and does not include irregular withdrawals from IRAs, 401(k) plans, and other forms of savings. It thus understates the resources used for retirement consumption and overstates the role of Social Security. Nonetheless, these statistics on the absolute size of Social Security and on its relative share of retirement income indicate the importance of Social Security benefits to retirees.

Benefit adequacy is generally measured in relative terms by calculating a replacement rate, which is a ratio that compares the level of benefits in retirement to the level of the worker's preretirement earnings. The concept is based on the life cycle theory of consumption, which holds that people attempt to maintain their preretirement standard of living into retirement. Because retirees no longer save for retirement, they have access to a higher percentage of their income for consumption than they did before they retired. Thus they can receive lower income than their preretirement income and still maintain their standard of living.

Financial advisers generally measure the replacement rate as retirement income received in the first full year of retirement relative to preretirement earnings in the last year or last few years of work. It is often argued that a replacement rate of 70 percent is needed for most workers. A full discussion of what target replacement rates should be is beyond the focus of this book, but it should be noted that target replacement rates vary by income, being lower for higher-income persons. In addition, replacement rates don't work nearly as well as a measure of retirement income adequacy in a defined contribution environment, where pensions do not provide regular flows of income, as they did in a defined benefit plan environment, where pensions provided annuities (Hurd and Rohwedder 2015).

Confusing further the issue of the adequacy of Social Security benefits, Social Security calculates the replacement rate provided by Social Security benefits in a different way that is not directly comparable to the standard measure (Mitchell and Turner 2010, Biggs and Schieber 2014). Instead of price indexing earnings in calculating lifetime average earnings, Social Security wage indexes earnings. Because wages generally grow faster than prices, wage indexing results in a larger value for earnings in the denominator of the replacement rate than does price indexing, which results in lower calculated replacement rates. While Social Security calculates that a typical worker has a replacement rate of about 40 percent, Biggs and Schieber (2014), using the methodology generally used by financial advisors, calculate that the typical person retiring at age 62 receives a replacement rate of 52.

The replacement rate for a medium earner in 2002 using Social Security's method of calculating replacement rates was 39 percent, after deducting Medicare premiums. Deducting Medicare premiums is done to indicate the replacement rate that is available after that expense. By 2030, the replacement rate will fall to 31 percent. The decline occurs because of the increase in the normal retirement age, because Medicare premiums will be higher, and because of the taxation of an increased share of Social Security benefits. The income floor below which Social Security benefits are taxed is not indexed, so that over time an increasing percentage of retirees have income above that floor and are thus subject to the tax (Reno and Walker 2013).

Because Social Security benefits increase when workers postpone their start date past age 62, up to age 70, benefit adequacy, measured by the level of annual benefits received, increases when a worker postpones the age at which he or she claims benefits. While the Social Security benefit formula links benefits to average wages, Social Security benefits will rise less rapidly over time than wages because of the effect of raising the normal retirement age from 65 to 67, which is currently being phased in. That change acts as a benefit cut, reducing benefits at any age they are claimed, relative to what they would have been. When the normal retirement age was 65, benefits received at age 62 were 80 percent of the full amount (the Primary Insurance Amount or PIA). When the normal retirement age reaches 67, which is for people born after 1959, benefits at age 62 will be 70 percent of the PIA, or a 12.5 percent benefit cut.

POLICY OPTIONS AND ISSUES

Benefit Cuts while Protecting Low-Income Workers

Social Security reform to restore solvency may involve benefit cuts. All of the Republican presidential candidates in 2016 who provided proposals for Social Security reform, except Donald Trump and Mike Huckabee, favored benefit cuts, either through raising the normal retirement age or through reducing the generosity of the benefit formula (Center for Retirement Research at Boston College 2015).

One extreme option for cutting benefits for higher-income retirees is to make Social Security means tested, by which only low-income persons would qualify for benefits. Alternatively, at the other extreme, means testing could be done so that only high-income persons didn't qualify for benefits. Of course, there is a range of options in between. Although means testing would make Social Security benefits more targeted, the justification for financing Social Security through the payroll tax would be diminished. In addition, means testing would introduce adverse incentives, as some people would reduce their economic activity to avoid being affected by means testing. Canada and Australia both have means tests that start at relatively high income levels. The income taxation of benefits for higher-income persons is an implicit form of means testing.

New Jersey Governor Chris Christie, a 2016 Republican presidential candidate, has proposed that Social Security benefits be reduced for seniors making more than $80,000 a year in non–Social Security income and be completely eliminated for seniors making more than $200,000 a year in other income. According to some estimates, if the income limits applied to individuals rather than households, the policy would result in about 2 percent of older persons losing all Social Security benefits (*Wall Street Journal* 2015).

A benefit cut through raising the normal retirement age would be an across-the-board benefit cut and thus would disproportionately affect the retirement income of low-income persons because they receive a higher percentage of their retirement incomes from Social Security. Many low-income persons rely on Social Security for a large share of their retirement income. In dealing with the issue of benefit cuts, Diamond and Orszag (2004) note that in their proposal, for an average earner retiring around 2070, benefits would be 18 percent lower than under the current benefit formula but would be roughly 50 percent higher in real terms (inflation adjusted) than for a new retiree currently because of the growth in real income over time.

Life expectancy indexing of benefits is an automatic way of cutting benefits over time to take into account the effects of increased life expectancy. In Sweden, life expectancy indexing of benefits is done by the use of an annuity divisor that reflects improvements in life expectancy at age 65. For each birth cohort, the annuity divisor adjustment is established at age 65, with a provisional adjustment made for retirements starting at age 61, which is the benefit entitlement age. No further reductions in benefits for improvements in life expectancy occur after the retiree reaches age 65.

Benefit cuts could be targeted by income by making changes in the benefit formula that was described in Chapter 1. Recall that there are three segments of the Social Security benefit formula. The first segment goes up to AIMEs of $856, or $10,272 a year. One approach would be to retain the benefits for people with earnings in that segment. In addition, for higher earners, benefits would be cut in a manner that increased in percentage terms as earnings increased. For example, if the benefit adjustment factor for the second segment was reduced from 0.32 to 0.26, a person with AIMEs of $4,000, or $48,000 annually, would have their benefits cut from $1,776.48 to $1,587.84, or a decline of 10.6 percent. If Social Security accounted for about half of that person's retirement income, her retirement income would decline by about 5 percent. Alternatively, only the benefit adjustment factor affecting the third segment of the benefit formula would be reduced, which only affects the top earners, approximately 15 percent of workers (Diamond and Orszag 2004).

The United Kingdom has cut benefits by increasing the number of years used in benefit calculations—20 percent of average lifetime earnings, rather than 25 percent of the average of the best 20 years of earnings.

Benefit Increases—Across the Board or Targeted?

Because of the relatively low level of generosity of Social Security benefits in the United States, compared to some other countries, some people have advocated for across-the-board benefit increases (Altman and Kingson 2015), despite the fact that Social Security is already facing a funding shortfall. In 2016, the only major presidential candidate favoring across-the-board benefit increases was Senator Bernie Sanders (D). As well as favoring benefit increases for all Social Security beneficiaries, he also favors an increase in the generosity of the cost-of-living adjustment by using the CPI for the Elderly. The Social Security Actuaries assume this would raise the price indexing of benefits in payment by 0.2 percent a year. In addition, he favors establishing a minimum Primary Insurance Amount of 125 percent of the poverty line for workers who have contributed to Social Security for 30 or more years (Goss 2016).

The issue of increases or cuts in benefits raises questions as to what should be the role of government versus individuals, families and employers in providing retirement income. A 2011 survey finds that 3 percent of Americans aged 25–59 expect there to be increases in Social Security benefits (Luttmer and Samwick 2015). While economics cannot provide answers to whether there will be increases or cuts, which ultimately is a political question, it can provide insights.

In microeconomics, also called price theory, prices play a key role in the decisions people make concerning allocating resources. The old-age dependency ratio (the ratio of retirees to workers) acts as an implicit or shadow price for Social Security benefits (Turner 1984). The old-age dependency ratio acts as a shadow price because it is the marginal cost to workers of increasing Social Security benefits.

With the price of benefits rising, it is likely that the share of Social Security in retirement income will fall (Doescher and Turner 1988). The changing demographics are not favorable to benefit increases.

The ratio of beneficiaries to covered workers acts like a "price" (or shadow price) for benefits, meaning the amount the average worker must pay in social security taxes to raise the average benefit level by one dollar (Turner 1984). For example, when 10 workers contribute for every social security beneficiary, a dependency ratio of 0.10, it costs each worker $0.10 to provide one dollar of benefits to each beneficiary. By contrast, when two workers contribute for every beneficiary, a dependency ratio of 0.50, it costs each worker $0.50 to provide a dollar of benefits. Thus, as the dependency ratio rises with population aging, the "price" of providing social security benefits also increases.

With this price, a simple demand-supply model can be developed. Generally, economics predicts that, because of the law of downward sloping demand curves, when the price of something increases, the quantity demanded falls. Thus, the increase in the shadow price of social security benefits means that workers would need to pay more in payroll taxes to provide the same level of benefits; thus, their demand for social security benefits would decline, which would reduce the level of benefits provided.

A related point is that demand is affected not only by prices but also by income, and with rising income people may wish to have more leisure, including spending a greater percentage of their life in retirement. In addition, workers have other intergenerational commitments, namely, to children for public expenditures on education, but those expenditures are much smaller than for Social Security.

Between 1970 and 2000, the growth rates in Social Security–covered workers and beneficiaries were roughly equal, implying no change in the old-age dependency ratio, and thus no change in the shadow price for Social Security benefits. However, between 2000 and 2030, according to the intermediate projection of the Social Security Administration actuaries, the number of beneficiaries will grow considerably faster than the number of covered workers (Table 3.1). That change places pressure on Social Security financing and thus strengthens the case for adopting an automatic adjustment mechanism. What would be the effects of Social Security benefits increases? Some studies suggest that at least to some extent, benefit increases would be offset by people decreasing their own savings for retirement (e.g., Lachowska and Myck 2015). The effect, however, may not be the same for all groups of workers. In particular, low-income workers with low savings, who arguably are the target group of such a policy, have little in the way of retirement savings to offset against. However, an offset can also occur through increased debt holdings, for example by having a larger mortgage.

Catch-Up Benefits

Workers aged 50 and older who participate in employer-provided pensions or Individual Retirement Accounts have the option to make additional contributions, called catch-up contributions, a concept that could be extended to Social Security. Workers age 50 and older could have the option of making extra voluntary contributions to Social

Table 3.1 Projected Percentage Change in Old-Age and Survivors Insurance (OASI) Covered Workers and Beneficiaries, Selected Periods, 1970–2030

Year	OASI covered workers (000)	OASI beneficiaries (000)	Ratio of beneficiaries to covered workers (%)
1970	92,788	22,618	24.4
2000	154,624	38,556	24.9
2030 (intermediate projection)	184,794	71,547	38.7
Percent change			
1970–2000	66.6	70.5	2.0
2000–2030	55.0	85.6	55.4

SOURCE: Author's calculations from Social Security Trustees (2008).

Security. They would contribute both the employer and employee share of the payroll tax—10.6 percent. Thus, for every $10.60 extra that a worker contributed, the worker would be credited for an extra $100 in Social Security earnings for that year, with the possibility of crediting up to the payroll tax maximum. The payment could be made through regular withholding, if the employer agreed to do that, or could be made at the time the person filed their income taxes.

Most civilian workers in the federal government can make voluntary contributions to increase their annuity benefit. In the United Kingdom, workers can make voluntary contributions to social security to receive credit for years in which they were not working, and thus to raise their social security benefits. Voluntary contributions only apply toward benefits for the basic benefit, which is not earnings related but is based on years of contributions (Government of the United Kingdom 2016). This feature allows workers more flexibility in planning for their retirement needs.

Lump Sum Benefits

Given the popularity of lump sum benefits with many workers, Social Security could start offering a lump sum benefit in addition to the traditional annuity. The lump sum benefit would be paid to workers who postponed retirement past 62 and who opted for it. Instead of receiving an increased annual benefit with postponed retirement, workers would receive the benefit they would have received if they had retired at age 62, plus a lump sum payment when they claimed benefits equal to the present expected value of the increase in future benefits (Maurer et al. 2016). This option might encourage some workers to postpone retirement. While in principle it would appear to be revenue neutral for Social Security, it would bring payments forward in time and cause Social Security to reach insolvency sooner. Some workers might take it because they are worried about the future finances of Social Security; others might take it because they have a relatively short life expectancy and think it is a better deal than taking the increased annual benefits. For that reason, adverse selection would result in an increase in benefit costs for Social Security.

An alternative to the proposal by Maurer et al. (2016) is to allow workers aged 62 and older who had worked at least 35 years to have their contributions invested in the Thrift Savings Plan for federal government workers, the military, and members of Congress. This alternative would allow workers to augment funded individual accounts, it would encourage workers to keep working, and it could provide a lump sum benefit without the problem of adverse selection. The employer share of the payroll tax would continue to be paid into the Social Security trust fund.

Protections for Women

Poverty at advanced ages is a substantially greater problem for nonmarried women, who have poverty rates at older ages that are roughly twice as high as for older people overall (Butrica, Iams, and Smith 2004). Because of this financial vulnerability, some Social Security reforms are designed specifically to help women, though in legislative language the proposals are gender neutral. For example, to receive benefits as a divorced spouse, a marriage must have lasted for at least 10 years. This protection, which benefits women more than men, could be extended on a reduced, pro rata basis to marriages that lasted 5–9 years.

In Germany, the social security benefit rights acquired during marriage are automatically evenly split 50-50 between the divorced couple, so the benefit rights for the lower-earning spouse depend on the length of the marriage. In the United States, for marriages lasting more than 10 years, the length of the marriage does not affect the amount of Social Security benefits received by a divorcee. The benefits the divorced spouse receives are based on the benefits earned by the other spouse, including benefits earned after the marriage ended.

Hillary Clinton, a 2016 Democratic candidate for president, favors targeted benefit increases that aim to reduce poverty at older ages. Her proposals include raising survivors benefits, which would primarily benefit older women. Widows aged 65 and older have substantially higher poverty rates than other groups that age. Women risk falling into poverty when their husbands die because of the reduction in Social Security benefits. For a two-earner couple, Social Security benefits can fall by as much as 50 percent. Because of economies of scale in household expenditures—such as for housing—a single person needs substantially more than half of the income of a married couple to enjoy the same standard of living of the married couple.

Clinton also favors a credit for persons who spend time out of the labor force caring for other persons. This credit would raise the Social Security benefits for those persons by raising their average earnings used to calculate their benefits (Clinton 2016). The person providing care would receive an earnings credit for years of caregiving, which would be a credit to their Social Security earnings record. In marriages in which the wife does not work out of the home, the spousal benefit serves somewhat the same function as the caregiver's credit. For women with substantial labor market work, a caregiver's credit would offset one of the penalties of time spent out of the labor force. Of course, the credit would also benefit men who take off time to care for someone. Contribution credits in the United Kingdom can be received for years spent taking care of a child or an older or disabled relative.

The caregiver's credit would help women and men who take time out of the labor force to care for someone, while not qualifying for spousal benefits, and thus reducing their own Social Security benefits. Barr (1993) notes that a caregiver's credit is part of the United Kingdom's social security program. One problem with such a program is verifying that care was actually provided. For young children, the need for care can be established solely based on their age. It is more difficult to establish the need for care for older persons, where age alone is not sufficient evidence.

Longevity Insurance Benefits

Reintroduction of a longevity insurance benefit as part of Social Security could be an important policy innovation, in particular because this benefit is generally not provided by the private sector. Longevity insurance benefits could be an important component of a policy to restore Social Security solvency, offsetting at older ages benefit cuts that may be part of a Social Security reform package (see Blake and Turner [2014]; Iwry and Turner [2009]; Turner [2013]; Turner and McCarthy [2013]; Weller [2016]). Longevity insurance benefits are part of the retirement income system in Ireland (Hughes and Turner 2015), China (Chen and Turner 2015), and Germany (Chen, Hughes, and Turner 2016).

The need for longevity insurance benefits arises because in the United States poverty rates increase at advanced ages. For example, in 2011 the poverty rate was 7.5 percent for people aged 65–69 but jumped to 10.7 percent for people aged 80 and older (Wu 2013). If measured more accurately, however, the increase in poverty at older ages is substantially greater.

The Supplemental Poverty Measure is designed to correct a number of shortcomings of the official poverty measure. For example, the official poverty measure is based only on expenditures on food, while the Supplemental Poverty Measure has a broader definition of essential purchases (Bridges and Gesumaria 2013). It provides a much different picture of poverty at older ages than does the official poverty measure (Table 3.2). While it exceeds the poverty measure by 1.0 percentage point for the population as a whole, for the age group 80+ it exceeds the poverty measure by 8.3 percentage points. Further, while the traditional poverty measure rises from 7.3 to 10.7 percent for the population aged 70–74 and 80+, respectively, an increase of 3.4 percentage points, the Supplemental Poverty Measure rises from 11.9 to 19.0 percent for the population aged 65–69 and 80+, respectively, an increase of 7.1 percentage points. Longevity insurance benefits would address this problem.

Table 3.2 Increasing Poverty Rate by Age Group at Older Ages, 2011

Age	Poverty rate (%)	Supplemental poverty measure (%)
60–64	10.8	n/a
65–69	7.5	11.9
70–74	7.3	13.9
75–79	10.0	16.9
80+	10.7	19.0

NOTE: NA = not available.
SOURCE: Bridges and Gesumaria (2013); Wu (2013).

In addition, as dramatic as the increase is in poverty at older ages, it understates the risk of falling into poverty at advanced ages because of survivorship bias, which occurs because people in poverty have higher mortality rates than do the rest of the population. Thus, if no one fell into poverty at advanced ages, then poverty rates would decline because of survivorship bias, but in fact they increase (Muller, Levin, and Turner 2016).

One reason there has not been a popular outcry for a longevity insurance benefit may be that the official poverty statistics considerably understate the problem of poverty at advanced ages. In addition, the group affected, people in their eighties, are generally not able to present the case for themselves. Furthermore, some people may implicitly accept that people at advanced ages have financial problems.

Longevity insurance benefits would be relatively inexpensive to provide. The ratio of the population 80+ to the population aged 18–64 is only 5.6 percent (Bridges and Gesumaria 2013), indicating a low "shadow price" for those benefits. The Social Security actuaries evaluated the longevity insurance benefit proposal of President Obama in his fiscal year 2014 budget. They find that such a proposal would raise the long-run actuarial deficit by 0.18 percent of taxable payroll (Social Security Office of the Chief Actuary 2013). Thus the benefit could be financed by a 0.09 percentage point increase in taxable payroll by the employee and employer. The increase in the payroll tax rate necessary to finance this benefit would probably be imperceptible to most employees and employers.

These benefits would start payment at an advanced age, such as 82. Future Social Security reforms may reduce the generosity of Social Security benefits to restore solvency. Most reform packages that cut social security benefits raise elderly poverty (Sarney 2008). Thus, to prevent a rise in elderly poverty, the generosity of some benefits will need to increase to provide better targeting to vulnerable populations. That goal could be achieved by providing longevity insurance benefits.

While the essence of longevity insurance benefits is that they start at an advanced age, they could be structured in different ways. To provide an indication of the range of options, three alternative proposals are provided here. First, longevity insurance benefits could be provided as a flat benefit to all Social Security beneficiaries starting at age 82. This approach would be progressive in that the percentage increase in benefits would be greater for people with a low level of benefits. Second, the benefits could be provided as a percentage increase in the Social Security benefits the person is receiving, with perhaps the percentage increasing above age 82. A disadvantage of this proposal is that people with higher wealth tend to live longer than people with lower lifetime wealth, so providing benefits solely based on age would disproportionately help people in the higher wealth groups. Third, a more complex proposal would provide longevity insurance benefits only to qualifying persons age 82 and older who had low Social Security benefits. For low-income persons, the effects of benefit cuts later in life when they are least able to work would be moderated by such a change. This policy shifts Social Security resources toward persons who are both old and have low incomes. When this policy is enacted within a fixed budget constraint, without enhanced financing for Social Security, it involves a transfer of resources from people who are relatively young (in their early or mid-sixties) and well off to people who are old and poor. It thus would improve the targeting of Social Security benefits.

President Obama, in his initial proposal for his 2014 budget, included a type of longevity insurance benefit in Social Security

(Office of Management and Budget 2013). That proposed benefit would start at age 76, would phase in for each recipient over a period of 10 years, and when phased in would provide a benefit equal to about a 5 percent increase in the recipient's Social Security benefits. President Obama made this proposal to offset benefit cuts at older ages resulting from introducing the chained CPI, arguably a more accurate way of measuring increases in consumer prices than the traditional CPI because it takes into account changes in consumer spending patterns that are caused by changes in relative prices. Its cuts, however, would have a cumulative effect that would grow over time the longer a person had been receiving Social Security benefits. Thus, it would result in the largest cuts in benefits for the oldest beneficiaries. Those cuts would have been offset to some extent at advanced ages by the introduction of the longevity insurance benefit.

Garnishment of Social Security Benefits

A topic often not considered when discussing Social Security benefits is the possible garnishment of those benefits. Nongovernment creditors cannot garnish a person's Social Security benefits to recover unpaid debt, but the federal government can. These debts include unpaid federal income taxes and unpaid student loans. For student loans, the government can take up to 15 percent of the Social Security benefit, so long as there is at least $750 a month remaining (Stinson 2015). With the growth in student debt, this may become an increasingly important issue in the future.

Individual Accounts

Some conservative politicians, economists, and policy analysts have taken an individualist approach to how retirement income should be provided, favoring individual accounts as part of Social Security. Individual accounts play a role in social security systems in some countries, including in Central and Eastern Europe (Szczepański and

Turner 2014b), the United Kingdom (Blake and Turner 2007), Japan (Turner, Watanabe, and Rajnes 1994), Sweden (Turner 2004), China (Chen and Turner 2014), Kenya (Kwena and Turner 2013), the Middle East (Lichtenstein and Turner 2002), and South America (Gillion et al. 2000).

Among the most recent advocates for this policy is Senator Rand Paul (KY), a 2016 Republican candidate for president (Craver 2015). The policy would reduce the Social Security benefits of those persons taking the option, and in exchange part of their retirement benefits would be financed by their individual accounts. One effect of such a policy is that by reducing contributions to Social Security, the financing for Social Security would worsen. The policy would also subject those benefits received from individual accounts to the risk of market downturn, as well as to the risks related to poor financial decision making by many people.

To provide retirement income for low-income workers adversely affected by a Social Security reform that involved benefit cuts, Mark Warshawsky, former treasury assistant secretary for economic policy, has advocated a voluntary individual account add-on to Social Security (see Goss, Wade, and Chaplain [2008] for a discussion of this proposal). With this add-on, for workers earning below a certain amount (for example, $40,000 in 2008), employers would automatically deduct 3 percent of an employee's salary and send it to the Social Security Administration to be invested in a voluntary individual account. The contributions would be voluntary in that workers could opt out. The accounts would be managed by a federal government agency, such as the Thrift Savings Board, which manages the federal Thrift Saving Plan, which is the 401(k)-type plan for most federal government workers.

In Sweden, which has mandatory individual accounts as a small part of its social security system, an unanticipated problem has been that many people have received poor financial advice for managing their accounts because of the conflict of interest that financial advisers have—the advice that provides the most income to the adviser is sometimes not the best advice for the client (Weaver and Willén 2014). This issue could also arise in the United States (see, for example, Shen and Turner [2016]; Turner, Klein, and Stein [2016]).

BENEFIT CLAIMING STRATEGIES

For some people, the decision of when to claim benefits can be separated from the decision to retire. Those people are predominantly people with higher incomes, who have sufficient savings that they can afford to retire without immediately receiving their Social Security benefits. In this case, the decision changes from a labor supply decision about when to stop work to a wealth maximization decision about when to claim Social Security benefits. Some advisers recommend that those with sufficient assets spend down 401(k) assets or other savings and delay claiming up to age 70. Doing so increases monthly benefit payments.

Despite the increasing labor force participation of women and the narrowing of the gender-wage gap, a majority of married women still receive most of their Social Security benefits based on their husband's earnings. Most husbands still work more years than their wives and have higher earnings (Henriques 2012). The pattern of earnings within marriages affects possible claiming strategies.

Claiming strategies for married couples need to take into account their effects on the benefits of the survivor. The survivor in a couple where both have worked in jobs covered by Social Security will receive the higher of the benefits they each would receive as an individual. For this reason, it may be particularly advantageous for the wife to claim benefits early and the husband to postpone claiming benefits to an older age. This strategy would increase the wife's survivor benefits, assuming she outlived her husband.

The Bipartisan Budget Act of 2015 ended two benefit claiming strategies that were not widely used but among policy experts were widely thought to be generous loopholes for married couples sophisticated enough to use them (Sullivan 2016). Since they no longer are available, understanding those options is not important. However, one of them is explained here to give an idea of why they were ended. Workers aged 65 or younger on April 30, 2016, will lose the ability to suspend their benefits while allowing their spouses to collect under the worker's earnings record. By suspending their benefits until a later date, they formerly were able to increase their future benefits because of the adjustment of benefits for postponed retirement. That strategy was called "file and suspend." It allowed a worker to benefit from postponed receipt of benefits while the worker's spouse was simultaneously receiving a spousal benefit based on that worker's earnings record.

CONCLUSIONS

Future changes in Social Security are likely to involve changes in benefits. This chapter argues that because of the effect of population aging on the shadow price of Social Security benefits, benefit reductions are far more likely than benefit increases. Adding a longevity insurance benefit starting at age 82 would be a targeted way of offsetting the adverse effects of benefit cuts for vulnerable persons at older ages. The shadow price of such a benefit would be low because of the low ratio of persons that age and above to persons of working age.

Chapter 4

Retirement Policy

This chapter discusses the issue of when to retire and start taking benefits, as well as reforms—such as a longevity policy—that would affect when people retire. It compares cross-sectional versus longitudinal standards for evaluating policies concerning retirement age and considers changes in the early retirement age, which currently is 62, and changes in the normal retirement age, which currently is rising to age 67. Changes in the normal retirement age, however, are not actually retirement policy but rather changes in the benefit formula.

THE SOCIAL SECURITY RETIREMENT AGE

Much of the policy discussion about the Social Security retirement age confuses two concepts. Social Security benefits can be claimed at age 62, which we refer to as the early retirement age, or simply the retirement age. The normal retirement age is referred to as the full retirement age, but neither of those terms is descriptively accurate, and both can be misleading—the age is not "normal" in the sense of what most people do, neither is it "full" in the sense of reaching the maximum benefit level with respect to age. It is a parameter in the benefit formula, and it is the age at which a worker can receive Social Security benefits that are not reduced for early retirement. While many analysts refer to the normal retirement age as the Social Security retirement age (for example, OECD [2015]), that use of language is misleading, since relatively few people retire at that age and everyone can retire at age 62.

The normal retirement age currently varies from age 65 to 67, based on year of birth—for workers born between 1943 and 1954 it is 66; for people born later, it rises to 67. Liebman, MacGuineas, and

Samwick (2005) suggest that the normal retirement age be raised to 68 as a step toward restoring solvency to Social Security.

Factors Affecting the Age at Which a Worker Claims Social Security Benefits

The most common age for taking Social Security benefits has been 62, though the percentage claiming at that age has declined over time, with more people taking benefits at later ages. Over time the percentage of men who claim benefits at age 62 has declined considerably, from 56 percent in the mid-1990s to 36 percent in 2016 (Munnell and Chen 2015).

Benefits increase when a worker postpones the start date for taking Social Security past age 62 up to age 70. However, for each year of postponement, the person receives benefits for one fewer year. Thus, the worker faces a trade-off, which depends on how long the person expects to live and on the interest rates at the time. The longer the person expects to live, the greater the number of years she will receive the higher benefit. Therefore, a person with shorter than average life expectancy may find it advantageous to claim early, while a person with longer than average life expectancy would tend to find it advantageous to postpone retirement and claim benefits at an older age.

The interest rate affects the present value of future benefits; the present value is higher when the interest rate is lower. With increased life expectancy and low real interest rates, postponing receiving Social Security benefits for many people is currently a good decision, at least in terms of increasing the lifetime value of their benefits. Life expectancy at age 65 was 13.9 years in 1950 and 19.1 years in 2010 (Table 4.1).

By delaying claiming, the individual receives a larger Social Security benefit for the rest of his life. Thus, delaying claiming has the effect of purchasing an increase in the annuity benefit. The cost of the purchase is the benefit lost by delaying. By delaying retire-

Table 4.1 Life Expectancy at Age 65 (expected years of life remaining), Select Years, 1950–2010

Year	Life expectancy (years)
1950	13.9
1960	14.3
1980	16.4
2000	17.6
2010	19.1

NOTE: Combined life expectancy for males and females.
SOURCE: Centers for Disease Control and Prevention (2011).

ment for a year, a worker gives up one year's worth of Social Security benefits. In exchange, the worker receives annual benefits that are 8 percent higher in real terms for the rest of the worker's lifetime.

For workers the trade-off between postponing benefit receipt an additional year and the increase in future annual benefits was actuarially fair at a time when life expectancy was considerably shorter than it is now. (Actuarially fair means that the expected present value of benefits would be the same whether the person claimed benefits at 62 or at a later age, up to 70.) The loss in benefits from postponing their receipt would be exactly offset by the increase in future annual benefits gained by postponing receipt. Because of the increase in life expectancy at older ages, it is now in the financial interests of many people to postpone benefit receipt. Doing so means that either the person continues working or is able to finance retirement before Social Security benefit receipt using other assets and sources of income.

For people without substantial other assets, which is most people, the decision of when to take Social Security benefits is tied to the decision of when to retire. Thus, it is not based solely on the age at which the expected present value of lifetime Social Security benefits would be maximized. The value to a worker of postponing receipt of benefits is based not only on the increase in the worker's own benefits but also on the increase in the value of spouse and survivor benefits, particularly for men, because their spouses are likely to receive those benefits.

Because people taking advantage of the generous adjustment for postponed retirement are primarily upper-income workers (Bosworth, Burtless, and Zhang 2016), this feature is regressive, meaning that it disproportionately benefits upper-income workers. For that reason, and because it would save Social Security money, the adjustment should be reduced so that it is once again actuarially fair. This change can be viewed as a technical correction and thus might be easier to enact on its own, without being part of a major reform package.

Research has also shown that many people have a low level of financial literacy relating to Social Security. In particular, they do not understand the effect of delaying claiming on their future Social Security benefits, and this lack of knowledge leads them to retire earlier than they otherwise would (Benítez-Silva, Demiralp, and Liu 2009).

The decision to retire is also affected by factors related to the work environment, such as the physical and mental difficulty of work; the pleasantness of the work environment, including relationships with supervisors; and the person's health. For some people, retirement may be more related to their nonwork activities, such as caring for another person, or the desire to pursue interests outside work. Munnell and Sass (2008) argue that some employers may be lukewarm to older persons working longer, and age discrimination may be a factor.

A recent survey asked retirees to rate the reasons they had retired (Garabato 2016). Notably, only 14 percent said it was due to their inability to continue performing their jobs. Because the survey was not limited to people retiring before age 62, presumably a smaller percentage of the total who had retired before age 62 retired for that reason. Also of interest, 24 percent said they retired because they had become eligible for Social Security (at age 62) or Medicare (at age 65).

Life expectancy varies greatly across income classes, a factor that complicates Social Security policy. Waldron (2007) has calculated projected life expectancy for males, comparing those in the bottom half of the lifetime earnings distribution to those in the top half (Table 4.2). Her findings show that analyses based on improvements in life

Table 4.2 Life Expectancy at Age 65 (expected years of life remaining), by Lifetime Earnings, Males, Select Years, 1977–2006

Year	Bottom half of lifetime earnings distribution	Top half of lifetime earnings distribution
1977	14.8	15.5
1987	15.3	17.5
1997	15.7	19.6
2006	16.1	21.5
Difference 1977–2006	1.3	6.0

SOURCE: Waldron (2007).

expectancy are misleading if they do not distinguish between those in the bottom half of the lifetime earnings distribution versus those in the top half of the distribution. In 1977, life expectancy at age 65 for the bottom half and the top half of the earnings distribution differed by less than a year (0.7 years). By 2006, the difference was greater than 5 years (5.4 years). Over this time period, life expectancy improved by 1.3 years for those in the bottom half and 6.0 years for those in the top half. In addition, Waldron (2013) presents evidence that mortality risk for men declines over the income distribution at least up to the eightieth percentile (the top 20 percent). Thus, any change in the early retirement age would be more adverse to lower- than higher-income people when viewed at a point in time.

A study by the National Academies of Sciences, Engineering, and Medicine (2015) finds that taking into account differences in life expectancy by income quintile, workers at even the lowest income quintile would receive higher expected present value of lifetime Social Security benefits by postponing receipt of benefits from age 62 to 64. This result arises because the increase in annual benefits with postponement is more than actuarially fair. Thus, a policy that raises the early retirement age to 63 with workers receiving the current increase in benefits with postponed retirement would on average raise both benefit levels and costs for Social Security. It should be noted that maximizing the wealth value of Social Security benefits is not the goal of individuals whose claiming age is tied to their retirement. Rather, individuals seek to maximize their expected lifetime utility, which also takes into account the value of leisure that results from retiring and receiving Social Security benefits at an earlier age, and the disutility (or utility) from an unpleasant (or psychologically rewarding) job.

LONGEVITY POLICY FOR SOCIAL SECURITY

Social Security policy would be improved by explicitly taking into account the increase in life expectancy over time, rather than doing so on an ad hoc basis. Social Security currently does not have a policy for dealing with the effects on its financing of increases in life expectancy. Even if Social Security were not projected to have insufficient funds based on current life expectancy, with the current benefit formula, which does not take into account demographic changes, continued increases in life expectancy would cause an insufficiency to occur in the future. Therefore, a practical reform proposal to maintain Social Security's solvency arguably should include an adjustment of Social Security for rising longevity.

With a longevity policy, all fixed ages in the Social Security program—the early retirement age, the normal retirement age, the age at which survivors benefits and spousal benefits can be received, and the age at which postponement of retirement no longer leads to higher benefits would periodically be adjusted upward to take into account improvements in life expectancy. In addition, the adjustment of benefits for postponed retirement would be changed to maintain actuarial fairness so that lifetime benefits would be the same whether the person took benefits immediately or postponed receipt.

Indexing Benefits

Public policy problems arise when a fixed retirement age is set in law, as is traditionally done, because of increases over time in life expectancy. While indexing benefits for changes in prices has long been an established practice, indexing benefits for changes in life expectancy is only starting to be recognized as a desirable policy option. In Sweden, social security benefits are indexed for changes in life expectancy, with the generosity of benefits for each new cohort of retirees being slightly reduced to take into account the longer time period over which the benefits would be received. In the United Kingdom, the earliest age for social security benefit receipt is being raised from 65 to 67, with the timing of the raise based on projected improvements in life expectancy, which might be called quasi-indexing, since it is not indexing based on actual changes in life expectancy but based on expected changes.

Normal Retirement Age

Several policy options exist with respect to raising the normal retirement age, which would effectively be a cut in benefits. However, in the real world of politics, communicating a more obscure cut in benefits, although lacking in transparency, may be a more effective way to enable the enactment of needed changes to Social Security. However, while people often do not seem to realize it is a benefit cut, they object to raising the normal retirement age as if it had an effect on the age at which they could retire. Although cutting benefits and raising the early retirement age are not popular options, considerations of popular perceptions may increase the chances of the normal retirement age making it through the political process into policy.

First, the normal retirement age could be raised on an ad hoc basis to a higher age. It was raised in the 1983 amendments to the Social Security Act; phased in with a long delay, the normal retirement age was raised from 65 to 67 and took full effect for people born in 1960 or later, who were thus age 23 at the time of the change. Making such a policy change with a long lead time is the result of forward-thinking policy. It provides the people affected with ample time to adjust their work and savings patterns.

Second, the normal retirement age could be indexed to rise as the life expectancy of retirees increases. The 1994–1996 Advisory Council on Social Security (1996) included such a measure in its recommendations. Doing so would gradually reduce the Social Security replacement rate over time. Recognizing the large differences in changes in life expectancy between higher- and lower-income retirees, this indexing could be based on the improvement for lower-earnings retirees. An advantage of this approach is that the changes would be known in advance and thus would pose less risk to workers. Third, the normal retirement age could remain fixed, with benefits indexed to life expectancy, so that benefits gradually decline as longevity rises for successive cohorts (Diamond and Orszag 2004).

Early versus Normal Retirement Age

Politically, raising the early retirement age seems to be more difficult than raising the normal retirement age, with some politicians and others expressing outrage at the idea. For more than 40 years, Social Security's early retirement age of 62 has been an important benchmark for workers considering retiring. To allow workers ample time to adjust their plans, if the eligibility age for Social Security were raised to 63, such a change would presumably occur with a long delay, possibly 20 years, and with a phase-in period.[1]

Comparing an increase in the early retirement age with an increase in the normal retirement age, instead of raising the early retirement age, the benefits receivable at that age could be reduced. Thus, raising the normal retirement age would have the advantage of preserving the option for people to continue taking benefits at the early age if they were willing to accept the penalty of reduced benefits.

If everyone were rational economic decision makers, raising the normal retirement age would be a better policy than raising the early retirement age. The disadvantage of this approach, however, is that some people take benefits at the earliest age, seemingly because they view that age as acceptable but without assessing the value of postponing benefits. Taking benefits at age 62 not only reduces the benefits of the primary worker and spouse, it also reduces the survivor's benefits.

Thus, the comparison of benefit cuts versus early retirement age increases depends at least in part on the assessment of how many people take benefits at age 62 because of myopia or their viewing it as the default age, rather than making a rational decision as to that being their best age for claiming benefits.

Precedents

Raising the early retirement age is a policy that can be supported by historical precedent both in the United States and internationally. In 1940 when Social Security first paid benefits, the earliest age at which workers could receive benefits was age 65. For more than 20 years, the earliest age at which men could receive Social Security benefits remained at 65. In 1961, the early retirement age for men was reduced to 62. The reduction for women had occurred five years earlier, in 1956.

An early retirement age of 63 has many international precedents. In Germany, for example, the early retirement age is 63 for people with 35 years of work and 65 for those with fewer years, both ages gradually rising over time. In the United Kingdom, it is currently 65 for men, with the age being raised over time to 65 for women, and both ages being increased to 67. In Switzerland it is 65 for men and 63 for women. In New Zealand, it is 65. In Ireland, it is 66 (Turner 2007).

The Nature of Work

The nature of work has considerably changed over time for U.S. workers. They have experienced a long-term trend away from physically demanding jobs, as jobs have switched in turn from agriculture to manufacturing, then to the service industry and to the knowledge sector. For example, between 1992 and 2002, both men and women workers aged 55–60 saw slight declines in the percent who reported jobs that required substantial physical effort most of the time. The decline was from 20 to 19 percent for men and from 21 to 17 percent for women (Johnson 2004). Some 62-year-olds are in poor health, and others have difficult job situations. For these people, continuing to work to age 63 may be difficult or impossible. Some people are counting the days until they reach age 62 and they can retire and take Social Security benefits. Others were laid off in their early sixties or late fifties and face age discrimination in trying to find another job.

A Reform Package

A reform that raised the early retirement age should be part of a package that addresses these concerns. A policy of raising the early retirement age would have less of a negative impact on older workers if it were part of a package to strengthen work options for older Americans (Chen and Turner 2007; Ghilarducci and Turner 2007). For people in poor health, Social Security offers disability benefits. As part of a reform that raised the early retirement age, the requirements for qualifying for disability benefits at age 62 could be loosened.

What about people in physically demanding jobs? The percentage of workers in those types of occupations has declined considerably over time. Some of those workers are covered by pension plans. For example, mine workers, steel workers, and auto workers generally belong to unions. Their jobs provide a pension, and they could retire and use their pension to help finance their living expenses until age 63. For people who were laid off in their early sixties, a reform that provided special unemployment benefits starting at age 62 could be part of a Social Security reform package. A government campaign to reduce age discrimination in employment at older ages could also be part of a reform package. In addition, the package could include increased resources for job retraining of older workers. Thus, a reform that raises the early retirement age should include programs that would offset the hardship that it causes for some people.

Policy Evaluation

One approach to evaluating an increase in the early retirement age is to estimate how many people would be adversely affected by such a change. From an insurance perspective, everyone would be adversely affected because they would lose the insurance aspect of having the option of retiring early, even if it turned out that they did not need it. A different, and arguably better, approach than this cross-sectional approach, which is based on the effect on the population at a point in time, is one that looks at the cross-section over time. Thus, the question is not, how many people would be adversely affected by raising the early retirement age? The better question is, compared to 1990 (or some point in the past), would more people be adversely affected by an early retirement age of 63 now than were adversely affected by an early retirement age of 62 in the past? That comparison of cross-sectional equity in an intergenerational framework is an arguably better comparison because it puts the comparison in the historical context of intergenerational equity. For example, it could be framed as whether an early retirement age of 63 in the future would adversely affect more people than did an early retirement age of 62 for our parents or grandparents.

Changes in lifetime Social Security benefits and changes in annual benefits both have policy and welfare implications. Changes in lifetime benefits affect the wealth value of Social Security. Changes in annual benefits more directly relate to measures of the adequacy of Social Security, such as the replacement rate and the poverty rate. These changes can be viewed from different perspectives.

When taking the societal perspective and viewed over time, with no change in Social Security, including no change in annual benefits, lifetime benefits increase over time because of the increase in life expectancy. This change occurs both for high- and low-income workers because life expectancy has increased over time for both groups. Both annual benefits and lifetime benefits could be maintained if the Social Security early retirement age were increased over time to offset the effect of increases in life expectancy on lifetime benefits.

Fairness to Low-Income Workers

Low-income workers have on average a shorter life expectancy than high-income workers, and thus an increase in the early retirement age constitutes a greater percentage decline in their years in retirement than it does for high-income workers. This argument views the change at a point in time, rather than in the broader framework that includes considering changes in life expectancy over time. Economists have generally moved from point-in-time analyses to life cycle analyses.

Under a life cycle analysis, when the worker begins work, say at age 22, the worker has an expectation of a future Social Security benefit. When the worker retires more than 40 years later, the value of the promised benefit he or she receives has increased considerably, owing to the increase in life expectancy that has occurred over that 40-year period. Raising the early retirement age to take into account that increase in life expectancy would not constitute a reduction in lifetime benefits from the perspective of the worker beginning work; it would merely offset the increase due to rising life expectancy over the period.

Addressing the issue of cross-sectional equity, a simulation study has examined the distributional effects on people of raising the Social Security early retirement age from 62 to 65 (Mermin and Steuerle 2007). That study finds that workers in all income quintiles would receive lower lifetime Social Security benefits. However, workers in the lowest income quintile are least affected as a group, in part because a higher percentage of them receive Social Security disability benefits.

Bosworth, Burtless, and Zhang (2016) argue that the early retirement age should not be increased in line with the increase in average life expectancy because of the large difference between the increase in life expectancy for the bottom half of the income distribution as compared to the top half. As noted in Table 4.2, life expectancy for men has increased considerably more for those in the top half of the lifetime earnings distribution, compared to the bottom half. For the bottom half, life expectancy at age 65 increased by 1.3 years for the 29 years between 1977 and 2006. Consider a proposal that would raise the early retirement age to 63 in 20 years. Thus, even for those in the bottom half of the lifetime earnings distribution, that proposal would involve an increase in the early retirement age that was less than half the increase in life expectancy.

FLEXIBLE NORMAL RETIREMENT AGE

Increasing the normal retirement age while holding the early retirement age fixed would reduce Social Security's benefit costs. A possible policy to maintain replacement rates is to raise the early retirement age to offset the effect of benefit cuts on annual benefits. A flexible normal retirement age is an alternative policy that could preserve or even enhance the progressivity of Social Security benefits. Social Security policy could use the AIME to target policies that are more equitable for people with both lower lifetime income and lower life expectancy. However, while life expectancy is strongly correlated with AIME for men, it is only weakly correlated for women, and when pooling the genders the correlation disappears (Monk, Turner, and Zhivan 2010).

Alternatively, targeting could be done by the max AIME, which is the AIME for single persons and the maximum of the husband's or wife's AIME for married couples. Monk, Turner, and Zhivan (2010) find that the max AIME, which is a household measure of lifetime income, could be used for constructing a flexible normal retirement age because it is negatively correlated with mortality risk and also negatively correlated with other measures of economic vulnerability or inability to work at older ages. With a flexible normal retirement age, individuals in households with a low max AIME would have a lower normal retirement age than other individuals. This policy provides one way of dealing with the large differences in life expectancy by level of income.

Framing

One policy option that derives from the insights of behavioral economics has to do with the framing of different ages at which benefits can be claimed. The Social Security Administration uses the concept of the normal retirement age or full retirement age, but this concept has little to no economic content. Continued work or postponement of benefit receipt past that age results in further increases in benefits up to age 70. Nonetheless, some people appear to be confused by the normal retirement age, with a bunching of retirements at that age suggesting that there is something "normal" about retiring at that age. Dropping that concept, or instead calling age 70 the full retirement age, would have no effect on the calculation of benefits, but it could result in some people working longer and would reduce confusion.

Raising the Number of Years Counted in the Calculation of Social Security Benefits

Currently, 35 years of work are counted in the calculation of Social Security benefits. People who work longer careers must still pay the Social Security payroll tax, but they receive no benefit for years outside the 35 counted in the benefit calculation. This cap on countable years of work provides a disincentive to working a long career and is counter in its effect to the goal of encouraging people to postpone retirement ages.

This problem can be dealt with in different ways. First, workers who have worked 35 years since age 21 and who are 62 or older could be exempt from paying the Social Security payroll tax. Since there may be an advantage to some workers in dropping out low-earnings years in the benefit calculation because those years would reduce their AIMEs, it might be better to have the payroll tax end after 38 years of covered work. Second, the number of years counted could be extended to, say, 38. This approach could adversely affect some women, who tend to have shorter working careers than men because they are more likely to take time off from paid work to care for children. To the extent that those women receive benefits based on their husband's earnings, rather than their own, they would not be affected by this change, so this point may not be particularly strong. Counting more years in the benefit formula would reduce benefits because the extra years would be years of lower earnings. Third, the benefit formula could be changed so that workers would build up credits toward benefits, and they would receive credits for each year worked. This approach involves the most dramatic change in the way benefits are calculated, but it also appears to be the best approach in terms of both fairness and incentives.

An alternative would give credit for all work above 38 years through a new benefit, with no change in the current benefit formula. This proposal would create a Notional Defined Contribution (NDC) system for work above 38 years. With an NDC system, each worker working more than 38 years would have a notional account to which his payroll tax payments would be credited. Each worker would be given interest credit on the account, so although the account would appear to be similar to an individual pension account, it would be unfunded. This approach would provide credit for long careers, but with no change in the existing benefit formula. The extra taxes they paid would be credited to the NDC system, so they would not be penalized as they currently are for long careers. A variant of this policy could be to have funded rather than notional individual accounts, with the accounts invested in the Thrift Savings Plan, which is the 401(k)-type plan for federal government workers.

CONCLUSIONS

A number of different aspects of Social Security policy with respect to retirement age have been discussed in this chapter. Retirement age policy affects benefit adequacy, the fairness of the distribution of benefits, and the cost of providing Social Security benefits. Increases in life expectancy have raised the cost of lifetime benefits. One policy option for Social Security would be to develop an explicit policy dealing with the effects on Social Security of increasing life expectancy. Raising the early retirement age to 63 should be done with a long lead time and a phase-in period.

Raising the early retirement age is a policy that can be supported by historical precedent in the United States. In 1940, when Social Security first paid benefits, the earliest age at which workers could receive benefits was age 65, and it remained that way for more than 20 years. In 1961, the early retirement age for men was reduced to 62. The reduction for women had occurred five years earlier, in 1956.

Note

1. See Turner (2007) for international experience with such a policy.

Chapter 5

Reforming the Reform Process

Neither Medicare nor Social Security can sustain projected long-run program costs in full under currently scheduled financing, and legislative changes are necessary to avoid disruptive consequences for beneficiaries and taxpayers. If lawmakers take action sooner rather than later, more options and more time will be available to phase in changes so that the public has adequate time to prepare. Earlier action will also help elected officials minimize adverse impacts on vulnerable populations, including lower-income workers and people already dependent on program benefits.
—Social Security Trustees (2014)

To do nothing is within the power of all men.
—Samuel Johnson (1709–1784)

$\mathbf{A}$s the Social Security Trustees have emphasized in their annual reports for more than a decade, Social Security should be reformed as quickly as possible because needed reforms are less drastic if they are done without further delay. In 2015, Congress made a few technical reforms to Social Security—it dealt with the impending shortfall of the Disability Insurance trust fund but did not address Social Security's financing problems. The 2015 Social Security reforms were a missed opportunity by Congress. Realistically, under the current system of policymaking, Social Security reform done years before a crisis is not likely to happen.

KICKING THE CAN DOWN THE ROAD

Given that Congress has a long tradition of kicking the can down the road when it comes to Social Security reform, this chapter discusses two approaches for reforming the Social Security reform process. First, it considers automatic adjustment mechanisms, such as those that were adopted in Sweden. Second, it applies the concept of defaults to deal with inertia in Congress concerning enacting Social Security policy to restore solvency. That proposal is based on experience in Canada and Japan with policies that help maintain the solvency of social security in those countries.

This chapter presents a measure of policy inertia that we use to compare inertia across countries and examines policy in Canada and Japan that provides lessons concerning our proposal for the use of defaults. The chapter also discusses the option of automatic policy adjustments, which has been enacted by about a dozen countries.

While Social Security reform traditionally has been framed as the choice between the unpopular changes of tax increases and benefit cuts, from the perspective of the costs of policy inertia, a benefit of Social Security reform is that it resolves the uncertainty people face about what their future benefits and taxes will be.

POLICY INERTIA: COSTS AND CAUSES

Policy inertia is the failure to change public policy in the face of incentives or the future necessity to do so. Although it has been known for considerably more than a decade that Social Security is insufficiently funded for the long run, Congress has not made a single substantial change to address this issue. The goal of responsible policy making ideally would have provided the incentive for action. Because the need for change is not immediate, and because the problem can be solved only with unpopular changes, politicians are hesitant to take action.

The longer the delay in enacting reform, the larger the tax increase or benefit cut—the changes would be spread over fewer cohorts of workers, and there is less time for interest to accumulate. If delayed to the last moment, the required increase in the payroll tax rate—if that were the sole change—would be 4.4 percent compared to an increase of 2.7 percent had the problem been addressed 20 years earlier (Committee for a Responsible Federal Budget 2013).

Policy inertia concerning Social Security is not due to a lack of awareness of the problem, nor is it due to a lack of awareness of the consequences of delay. As the statement by the Social Security Trustees cited above indicates, policy experts have been arguing for a need to address the issue of Social Security solvency on a timely basis.

The policy uncertainty relating to Social Security is one of the largest sources of policy uncertainty for American workers (Luttmer and Samwick 2015). It makes it more difficult for workers to plan how much they need to save for retirement and when they can afford to retire. Workers have limited ability to insure against these policy risks and thus can mitigate them only by engaging in costly precautionary behavior in the form of increased savings and postponed planned retirement. Since those activities are difficult for many workers, they face the risk of having a diminished standard of living in retirement.

The life cycle model in economics argues that workers wish to smooth their consumption over time. Social Security policy inertia makes it difficult for them to do that. Luttmer and Samwick (2015) empirically analyze the magnitude of these effects, concluding that American workers on average would be willing to accept a 4–6 percent benefit cut if that would remove the policy uncertainty.

Policy inertia and the resulting insufficiency of Social Security's funding may contribute to a lack of confidence in Social Security. The EBRI Retirement Confidence Survey in 2015 finds that 19 percent of people aged 25–69 believe they will get nothing from Social Security, presumably because of its inadequate financing. That figure is up from 10 percent in 1991 (EBRI 2015).

Policy inertia is also costly to the federal government. Since 2010, Social Security's benefit payments have exceeded its payroll tax receipts (plus taxes paid on Social Security benefits), causing Social Security to have a negative effect on the government's cash flow (Congressional Budget Office 2015a).

The consequences for such inaction are serious. The last major policy changes to Social Security, in 1983, were made in a crisis at the last moment, with only weeks to spare before benefit payments would be delayed because of insufficient funds (Light 2005). The same thing nearly happened with the Disability Insurance Trust Fund, which was scheduled to have insufficient money in 2016 but was saved by a short-term fix in 2015. As of 2016, with 18 years to financial insufficiency, the next reform of Social Security OASI may also occur at the last moment. The reform process isn't working.

PREVIOUS STUDIES

The concept of inertia has been used in the context of lack of change by 401(k) participants in their participation or lack of participation in 401(k) plans (Choi et al. 2002; Madrian and Shea 2001; Muller and Turner 2013). Turner and Klein (2016) discuss policy inertia in the context of the benefit eligibility age for Social Security and the Military Retirement System. They note that policy inertia with respect to adjusting those benefit eligibility ages is considerably greater in the United States than in several other countries.

Hoskins (2010) discusses whether the use of the 75-year projection period for evaluating Social Security financing is a factor in policy inertia in the United States. He notes that the United States is an outlier with respect to the length of its actuarial projections, with Germany requiring projections of 15 years, and several European countries, including France, requiring projections of 30–40 years. Japan, however, uses actuarial projections of 95 years. He raises the question of whether a shorter time horizon might result in more frequent reforms in some countries.

The idea that Social Security reform must achieve adequate funding for 75 years and beyond raises the hurdle as to the type of changes that policy analysts consider to be acceptable. For example,

Brandon (2014) presents potential Social Security fixes but focuses entirely on fixes required to return solvency for the 75-year horizon. A shorter projection period would presumably facilitate reform because reforms could be made in smaller increments. One measure of the adequacy of Social Security's financing is its annual cost ratio. The Social Security annual cost ratio is the ratio of the cost of the program, mainly benefit payments, to taxable payroll. Because the long-run trend of the cost ratio is upward, reforms for longer time periods must involve larger changes. Reforms for shorter time periods can be incremental.

POLICY INERTIA: AN INTERNATIONAL COMPARISON

Although no major changes have been made in Social Security since 1983, a measure of policy inertia that is comparable across countries is the number of years since the early retirement age was changed. Since 1961, the early retirement age for men in the United States has been 62. Many countries have raised the benefit eligibility age for social security because of increasing longevity. Table 5.1 provides the date of the last change in the benefit eligibility age for social security pension in selected countries. The sample of countries is a convenience sample and thus is not a representative selection of a scientifically selected population. Nonetheless, it provides examples of a number of countries, many of which are similar in important ways to the United States. Using that table, policy inertia can be measured as the number of years since a change in the benefit eligibility age, with 2015 being the base year. With the exception of China, which has announced its intention to raise the benefit eligibility age in the near future, the United States has the highest measure of policy inertia among these countries. For example, while it was 54 years since the benefit eligibility age was raised in the United States (as of 2015), it was 28 years since the benefit eligibility age was raised in Canada.

Table 5.1 Year of Last Change in Social Security Benefit Eligibility Age, Selected Countries, 2015

Country	Year of last change in social security benefit eligibility age	Inertia index: 2015 (average number of years since last change for social security pensions)
United States	1961	54
China	1951	64
Canada	1987	28
Sweden	1998	17
Ireland	2015	0
Poland	2015	0
France	2015	0
United Kingdom	2015 (women only)	0

SOURCE: Turner and Klein (2016).

One possible explanation for the high degree of inertia in the United States compared to the other countries in Table 5.1 is that all the other democracies listed in the table have parliamentary governments. Political commentators argue that a weakness of the presidential form of government is political gridlock (Brady and Volden 2006). With a parliamentary government, when the ruling party has a majority in Parliament, it is relatively easy to pass legislation that the prime minister wants. That would be similar to a situation where the president and the majority party in both the House of Representatives and the Senate are from the same party, which is relatively uncommon in the current era in which the Democrats and Republicans are relatively equal in electoral strength.

AUTOMATIC ADJUSTMENT MECHANISMS

Reforms are much easier to enact when benefits are being raised than when benefits are being cut. In the age of social security retrenchment, some countries have adopted automatic adjustment mechanisms because of the difficulty the political system has in enacting unpopular reforms. These mechanisms automatically change the social security program parameters in a predetermined way, depending on economic and demographic developments. For example, these policies decide in advance how Social Security will be reformed to deal with the added costs resulting from life expectancy increases. Automatic adjustment mechanisms address the interrelated problems of social security sustainability; the political difficulty for politicians of reforms that involve retrenchment; and the political risk to workers, retirees, and employers associated with ad hoc social security reforms, which are difficult for workers to plan for because the changes are not known in advance.

Recognizing the difficulties politicians have in enacting unpopular reforms during this time of population aging, at least 12 countries have adopted life expectancy indexing of social security benefits or automatic adjustments tied to an indicator of social security insolvency (Turner 2011). Both types of reforms provide automatic adjustment mechanisms for sustaining the solvency of social security systems and reducing the political risks for workers and beneficiaries. Automatic adjustments are generally small, frequent, and predictable—all desirable features. Automatic adjustments are transparent. It is clear how adjustments will be made and who will bear what costs when an adjustment occurs.

With automatic adjustments to benefits, taxes, or the early or normal retirement age, increases in life expectancy automatically lead to program parameter changes. However, the adjustment mechanisms used for indexing can vary.

The differences in automatic adjustment mechanisms can be categorized in four dimensions:

1) the frequency of the adjustment,
2) the triggering event,
3) whether the trigger is a hard trigger or a soft trigger, and
4) the change that is triggered.

First, some automatic adjustments annually test for the need for change and make any necessary changes; these adjustments are designed as part of the ongoing financing to maintain the solvency of a system. For example, life expectancy indexing of initial benefits generally is done annually, as in Sweden, but Italy adjusts benefits every three years.

Second, the social security system's choice of triggering event varies. Some adjustments are tied to the system's underlying economics and demographics, such as changes in life expectancy, the old-age dependency ratio, or real wages. Others are tied to a measure of the insolvency of the system, and adjustments are made only if the system is judged not to be fully solvent over the long run.

Third, the trigger can be a "soft" trigger, meaning that the government must do something to resolve the problem but may choose among different measures. Alternatively, it can be a "hard" trigger, meaning that the government's adjustment is predetermined and automatic (Penner and Steuerle 2007). In most countries that adopt automatic adjustment mechanisms, the trigger is a hard trigger if the adjustment involves life expectancy indexing of benefits. However, triggers tied to a measure of insolvency are generally soft triggers, with some degree of political involvement in the process. Even in Sweden, which has a hard trigger with respect to insolvency, the government maintains oversight, so the automatic adjustment may be overridden.

Fourth, the change that is triggered can be an adjustment in tax rates, benefits, retirement ages, or some combination.

In the past, the United States has made ad hoc reforms to maintain the solvency of Social Security. Ad hoc reforms require elected officials to enact legislation each time an adjustment to social security financing is needed. These reforms have a high degree of political risk for workers because their timing and magnitude are unknown in advance. While it is often argued that Social Security benefits are less subject to risk than are benefits financed through individual accounts, the political risk workers face due to ad hoc reforms can be sizable. The distributional consequences across workers are unknown in advance and depend on whether benefits are cut, taxes raised, or both. Because of the political difficulty in legislating cutbacks in social security programs, ad hoc reforms tend to occur in a crisis, with little advance notice to workers and retirees as to the legislated changes. They thus may create hardships for workers nearing retirement, who are facing less generous Social Security benefits than they had planned for.

Automatic adjustment mechanisms can eliminate the need for large program changes negotiated in a crisis. They can greatly reduce the risk of insufficient financing, but they, however, do not eliminate all risk. Workers still face the risk that benefit levels may be reduced, taxes raised, or retirement ages moved back. Risk is reduced in that workers know under what circumstances such changes will occur. Political risk may be reduced with automatic adjustment mechanisms, but it is generally not eliminated, as politicians can always intercede and modify the changes that were designed to be automatic—this has happened in Sweden and Germany. In Sweden, the financial crisis and recession led to a decline in the value of accumulated contribution surpluses held in buffer funds that was expected to lead to a reduction in benefits in 2010. This step was avoided when a multiparty working group agreed to a change in the social security law that would base the activation of the automatic balancing trigger on buffer fund balances (formerly a single year) to a three-year average (Bosworth and Weaver 2011). As a consequence, future benefit cuts resulting from swings in fund balances would be moderated.

In Sweden, with the automatic balancing mechanism to maintain solvency, if the growth rate of real per capita wages is constant at 1.6 percent per year, the social security benefit is adjusted solely by changes in the CPI. If the annual growth rate of real per capita wage income falls below 1.6 percent, however, the cost of living adjustment is less than the increase in the CPI, and if the growth rate of real per capita wage income exceeds 1.6 percent, the adjustment is greater than the CPI. For example, if the annual growth rate in real per capita wages were 1.5 percent, the increase in benefits in payment would be 0.1 percent less than the rate of growth of the CPI.

Real per capita wage growth in Sweden has averaged about 2 percent over long periods (Palmer 2000). Because this average rate exceeds the rate of 1.6 percent in the adjustment formula, over time this indexing of benefits is expected to be more generous than price indexing based on the growth in the CPI. Thus, Swedish pensioners share with workers in the fluctuations and the long-term growth of the economy. However, in an economic recession, indexed benefits of Swedish pensioners will be lower than the level provided by price indexing, resulting in a reduction in real (price indexed) benefits.

Weaver and Willén (2014) conclude, after studying the Swedish social security reform of the late 1990s, that reform may be easier to enact when it is complex and opaque and thus not well understood by the electorate. They also argue that automatic adjustment mechanisms are likely to be effective when the adjustments are small and done frequently, so that their effects are less noticeable. The Swedish experience also indicates that politicians are unlikely to accept automatic adjustments that involve cuts in nominal benefits, which were overridden by the Swedish parliament.

Automatic adjustment mechanisms, however, while a step in the right direction toward maintaining sustainability, are themselves not necessarily financially sustainable. If they are not consistent with the fundamental principles of sustainability explained in Chapter 2 they will eventually need to have further adjustments.

POLICY LESSONS FROM JAPAN AND CANADA

Japan

In Japan, a special commission reviews the social security programs every five years. While reforms are not a mandatory outcome of this review process, that is the expectation and the tradition in

Japan (Liu 2000). Thus, historically, Japan has had relatively frequent, incremental reforms, which arguably are easier to enact than infrequent, major reforms. The current reality, however, is more complex. With population aging increasing the difficulty of reforms, more recently, Hayashi (2012) argues that in the face of unpopular needed reforms and the lack of an institutional requirement for reform, the Japanese government has a history of inertia.

Canada

The Canada Pension Plan (CPP) is Canada's social security program, except for the Province of Quebec, which maintains a similar but separate plan. The CPP is designed so that an established fund is expected to be adequate to cover the retirement of the Canadian baby boom and the aging of the population. There likely will not be a need for further contribution rate increases or benefit cuts over the next 75 years. However, a prolonged period of adverse financial markets, or other economic or demographic changes that are adverse to the solvency of the fund, could result in the need for changes to maintain solvency.

Every three years, the CPP's chief actuary evaluates the financial sustainability of the system. If the chief actuary determines that the system is not financially sustainable for the following 75 years, legislation passed in 1997 requires an automatic adjustment (American Academy of Actuaries 2002). The automatic adjustment occurs, however, only if the Canadian parliament cannot first decide on an adjustment, which is considered to be unlikely. The automatic adjustment freezes benefits for three years and increases the contribution rate in a single step for three years, until the next triennial evaluation of the fund. So far, insufficient funding has not been projected, so this mechanism has not been called upon.

THE PREDICTABLE CRISIS

Social Security policy making can be analyzed as a Tobit problem, similar to the purchase of a car, which also tends to be done infrequently and as a major purchase. The essence of the Tobit problem is that there is a relatively high hurdle for a minimum change, and for that reason change is made infrequently. In the case of Social Security, the high hurdle is the tradition that changes need to restore solvency for 75 years.

A major difference from the typical Tobit problem, such as purchasing a car, is that the longer Congress waits, the more expensive is the action required. Delay raises the hurdle for policy change by increasing the required level of benefit cuts or tax increases. This effect raises the likelihood of Social Security changes being made due to a crisis. Congress does not deal with the problem until a crisis forces politicians to act.

CHANGING CHOICE ARCHITECTURE TO OVERCOME POLICY INERTIA: USE OF DEFAULTS

An insight of behavioral economics is the use of defaults to overcome the inertia people sometimes experience and to result in desirable outcomes for them when otherwise they would not make a change. Inertia as a reason for workers not enrolling for pension coverage has been addressed by autoenrollment, where the default is that workers are automatically enrolled to participate in a 401(k)-type plan. For example, autoenrollment has been used in the Thrift Savings Plan for federal government workers as a way to increase the participation rate.

Inertia has been addressed in other contexts by the use of defaults. As explained in the previous section, defaults are used in Canada as part of their system for maintaining solvency of their social security program. That approach could be used to deal with inertia in U.S. Social Security policy.

Choice architecture refers to the way choices are framed. In Social Security policy, choices are framed as requiring action by Congress that restores solvency for Social Security for at least 75 years. The default for Social Security policy is that no action is taken until a crisis forces Congress to act. Social Security policy changes are made infrequently, generally in response to a crisis, and tend to be major changes.

My proposal has three parts: 1) the basic framework, 2) an example of a default reform proposal, and 3) a strategy for enacting the proposal.

The Basic Framework

The essential aspect of the proposal is that Congress makes a binding commitment to not let the date of Social Security insolvency be less than 15 years away. With this proposal, every time the intermediate projection of the Social Security actuaries indicates that there is insufficient financing for the next 15 years, Congress will be given one year to restore solvency for the following 20 years. If Congress fails to act within that time frame, automatic changes would restore solvency for 20 years. The package would involve several changes to Social Security, thus minimizing the effect of any single change. Because the changes are made years in advance, rather than at the last moment, and because they restore solvency for 20 years rather than 75 years, they would be smaller than would otherwise be necessary.

This proposal addresses inertia in part by lowering the hurdle so that reforms would be done as a series of relatively small reforms. Because the changes would be made 15 years in advance of the crisis instead of at the last minute, and because the requirement would be that Social Security would be solvent for 20 years rather than 75, the required changes would be considerably smaller.

The Default Reform

Solvency could be restored by equal measures of financing increases and benefit cuts. Luttmer and Samwick (2015) find that more than half of American workers (58 percent) expect that Social Security reform will involve both financing increases and benefit cuts, while 18 percent think that reform will mostly or entirely involve benefit cuts, and 24 percent think that it will mostly or entirely involve revenue increases. Thus, such a reform would be consistent with what the majority of Americans expect.

Under this reform proposal, financing increases would be divided equally between an increase in the maximum earnings subject to the payroll tax and an increase in the payroll tax rate. The benefit cuts would occur through an increase for future retirees in the normal retirement age and a six-month delay in the cost-of-living adjustment. While these changes appear to be balanced and reasonable, they are not ideal; rather, they provide Congress an incentive to make changes that it views are superior.

For the first time, Congress would be required to maintain its solvency, which could improve public confidence in Social Security. Under this proposal, solvency would be maintained through a series of small changes, unless Congress decided instead to make major changes. Social Security would be solvent for at least 15 years, and Social Security reforms would no longer be in a crisis mode, as they were in 1983.

This reform proposal would result in a different, arguably better, distribution of burden across generations than would a reform proposal that was enacted at the last minute. It would result in a more even sharing of burden across a larger number of cohorts. For this reason, it would provide a more equitable distribution of the burden across generations.

The last cohort of the baby boom generation was born in 1964 and thus turns 62 in 2026. If a reform occurred at the last moment, and if it did not affect the benefits of those already age 62, then the entire baby boom generation would be spared from bearing the burden of the reform, with the costs of the reform shifted to their children. By contrast, if the reform were done in 2016, a decade earlier, then tax hikes and benefit cuts would be borne by roughly half of the baby boom generation. Thus, this proposal would result in an arguably better intergenerational distribution of reform costs than a long-term reform done at the last minute.

Enacting the Proposal

The "save more tomorrow" concept means that people commit today to do something in the future (Benartzi and Thaler 2004). It is easier to commit to doing something in the future that a person is not inclined to do than actually taking that action in the present. By enacting this proposal in 2016, Congress would be committing to take action in 2020, according to the current Social Security Trustees report.

Financial Literacy and Social Security Reform

Ultimately, Congress is not acting on Social Security reform because no one is putting pressure on Congress to do so. Thus, this proposal has one additional part.

Financial literacy is of limited use for most people if they do not have a good idea of what their Social Security benefits will be. The Social Security Administration sends out projected benefit statements to people every five years—for example, at ages 25, 30, 35. However, these statements provide misleading information. They provide projected benefits based on the benefit formula in the current law. That information is misleading because Social Security is inadequately funded, and unless there is a reform, by law it will provide benefits only at the level that can be paid for—roughly a quarter less.

Social Security should amend its benefit statement and provide not only the current information but also the benefits that will be paid in the absence of reform. This will have two benefits: first, people will understand that there is a good chance they will not receive the higher level of benefits, and second, this understanding will likely cause people to pressure Congress to act.

This proposal is a second-best solution—it is better than simply waiting until a crisis happens. However, a better solution would be for Congress to enact a well-reasoned reform many years in advance of a crisis. One of the possible benefits of this proposal is that it might inspire Congress to take that route.

CONCLUSIONS

Social Security reforms will be less drastic if they are done without further delay; however, under the current system of policy making, realistically that is not going to happen. Social Security policy in the United States is characterized by a high degree of inertia.

Inertia has been addressed in other aspects of pension policy through defaults. I propose extending that insight to Social Security policy making. The essential aspect of the proposal is that Congress makes a binding commitment to not let the date of Social Security insolvency be less than 15 years away. With the proposal suggested in this chapter, every time the Social Security actuaries project that Social Security will have insufficient funding within 15 years, a package of small changes would occur that would restore solvency for the following 20 years. The package would involve several changes, thus minimizing the effect of any single change. Because the changes are made in advance, rather than at the last moment, and because they restore solvency for 20 years, rather than 75 years, they would be smaller than would otherwise be necessary. Congress would have the option to override the default by producing its own package that restored solvency for the following 20 years, but if it did not act, the default package would automatically take effect.

This proposal would help restore confidence in Social Security by assuring that the system would be solvent for at least 15 years. The proposal would also provide for reforms on a more timely basis than would otherwise occur. Also, the reforms would be predictable, unless Congress overrode them, in which case Congress would presumably provide reforms that were more politically appealing.

Chapter 6

The Way Forward

This book examines options for Social Security reform. It considers reforms that would restore solvency and reforms that would improve the way benefits are provided in regard to fairness and targeting. The book also proposes a reform of the reform process, presents a sustainable benefit formula, and argues that the increase in the shadow price of Social Security benefits makes an increase in benefits unlikely. It focuses on a number of prominent reform options, some that appear desirable and some that do not. This final chapter concludes by presenting a vision of the way forward.

ROADBLOCKS

Policy Inertia: Social Security's Biggest Problem

The biggest problem facing Social Security is Congress's failure to deal with its future insolvency. Social Security reform to restore solvency could occur in a responsible manner, through a reasoned process of political compromise that is done years before the date of insolvency—the earlier the reform is enacted, the less drastic the required changes will be.

An important aspect of financial literacy for workers, and thus financial advice, is understanding what future Social Security benefits will be. However, this is challenging because of the uncertainty about the nature and timing of future Social Security reforms. The information that the Social Security administration provides in its mailings to workers is highly misleading. The benefit projections assume that a future reform will provide sufficient revenue so that there will be no cuts in future benefits, and the projections do not disclose this key assumption. The disclosures should include projections of benefits actually payable in the absence of future reforms. The actual level of future benefits presumably lies between those two estimates.

Status Quo Bias

Social Security reform requires difficult choices. Is it possible to enact reform without causing hardship for anyone? A reform package likely will involve some combination of benefit cuts (such as raising the normal retirement age), payroll tax increases (such as raising the taxable maximum earnings), and possibly an increase in the early retirement age, all of which make people worse off. However, compared to doing nothing, which would result in automatic benefit cuts, the reform package is clearly an improvement. False comparisons are often made in policy discussions—in this case, if the status quo is maintained with no benefit cuts, no payroll tax rate increases, and no change in the early retirement age, then it is clear that the reform package would result in hardship. That approach could be called status quo bias in policy analysis. Any change in Social Security policy needs to be evaluated against the policy reform alternatives, rather than the status quo.

OPTIONS FOR A BALANCED REFORM

Social security reforms are usually introduced by countries as a package, involving a number of changes implemented simultaneously. This book provides suggestions for a balanced reform. Rather than needing to restore solvency for 75 years, as has been the goal traditionally (Diamond and Orszag 2004), the package could be designed to restore solvency for a shorter period, such as 20 or 30 years.

Revenue Reforms

Revenue reforms would include a small increase in the payroll tax rate and an increase in the taxable maximum earnings ceiling. Raising the payroll tax ceiling would bring a higher percentage of age-earnings into the Social Security earnings pool. The evidence from the increase in the Social Security payroll tax rate following its temporary decrease a few years ago suggests that a small increase in the payroll tax rate, shared equally by workers and employers, would go largely unnoticed if it were part of a reform with bipartisan support.

The percentage of Social Security benefits that are taxed for higher-income retirees could be raised to 100 percent (the percentage of benefits subject to tax), which would also have a small effect of improving the progressivity of the Social Security program, which has been adversely affected by the large increase in life expectancy for higher-income retirees relative to lower-income retirees. As it is currently, the large difference in mortality between higher- and lower-income persons is an element that favors higher-income persons in the receipt of lifetime benefits.

Another way to raise revenue would be to invest 15 percent of the Trust Fund in the stock market. Though currently not in fashion, the idea of increasing revenues by investing part of the Social Security trust fund in the stock market is an idea that Canada has successfully implemented. Any policy analyst considering this idea would only need to look to our neighbor for evidence regarding its feasibility.

As was mandated for federal employees in the 1983 reform, all new state and local government employees should be covered by Social Security. This change would improve Social Security's financing in the short run, though in the long run additional benefits would need to be paid. This change would make Social Security a truly universal program, which would be desirable in terms of paying for the intergenerational transfers that were made to the first generation that suffered through the Great Depression.

As an added source of revenue, all "lost" 401(k)-type accounts would be transferred to the Social Security Administration. The original owner of the accounts would not lose his or her rights to those accounts and could claim them from Social Security, but it is likely that many of the accounts would ultimately revert to the OASI Trust Fund.

Benefit Reforms

Social Security already provides modest benefits compared to the benefit programs of many countries. Retirees, who can do little to offset any benefit cuts, would particularly suffer. For that reason, Social Security reforms involving benefit cuts should be enacted with a lead time.

One way to increase benefits may be to improve the financial literacy of workers as it relates to knowledge about Social Security. In particular, some people claim benefits earlier than they otherwise would, and therefore receiving lower benefits, because they do not understand that postponing benefit receipt leads to increased future benefits. Thus, the Social Security Administration may need different procedures regarding workers claiming benefits at age 62. A simple one would be to call age 62 the early retirement age. In addition, the Social Security Administration may need to provide better information to early claimants about the value of postponing benefit receipt.

Workers aged 50 and older could also increase their future Social Security benefits by making voluntary additional Social Security contributions, called catch-up contributions. They would contribute both the employer and employee share of the payroll tax—10.6 percent. Thus, for every $10.60 extra that a worker contributed, he would be credited for an extra $100 in Social Security earnings for that year, with the possibility of crediting up to the payroll tax maximum. The payment could be made through regular withholding, if the employer agreed, or could be made at the time the worker filed income taxes.

Workers aged 62 and older who have worked at least 35 years could opt to invest their contributions in the Thrift Savings Plan for federal government workers, the military, and members of Congress. The Thrift Savings Plan is a low-fee plan (less than three basis points), which is like a 401(k). This alternative would allow workers to build up funded individual accounts, it would encourage workers to keep working, and it could provide a lump sum benefit. The employer share of the payroll tax would continue to be paid into the Social Security trust fund.

In a time of financing shortfall, where the Social Security benefits of some future retirees will likely be reduced, in part to offset those reductions, there is a need to increase in a targeted way some of the benefits that Social Security provides. On net, these changes will lead to a Social Security program that better targets its benefits to those who need them, while at the same time retaining it as a universal program that benefits nearly all older Americans.

To deal with the sharp increase in poverty that occurs at advanced ages, a longevity insurance benefit would be established, providing benefits starting at age 82. This would be a relatively inexpensive benefit to provide. It could be instituted as part of a reform package that otherwise cuts benefits but not for people aged 82 and older. As the book documents, Social Security originally was structured like a longevity insurance program that only about half of workers survived to receive. With improvements in life expectancy and the reduction in the age at which benefits can be received—from 65 to 62—Social Security is now an earnings-replacement program with a relatively small longevity insurance component.

A minimum benefit could be established for long-career workers with 30 or more years of covered work. This benefit would provide better retirement income for the working poor. The generosity of survivors benefits should be increased, particularly for two-earner couples. A single person needs more than half of the income of a married couple. Under the current system for a dual-earner couple, Social Security benefits can fall by as much as 50 percent after the death of either spouse. Introducing a caregiver's credit would help women and men who take time out of the labor force to care for someone. For caregivers not qualifying for spousal benefits, time taken out of the labor force reduces their Social Security benefits.

Recognizing that the early retirement age for Social Security originally was 65, that life expectancy is substantially greater now than in 1940—even for people with low earnings—and that many countries similar to the United States have higher early retirement ages than does the United States, the early retirement age would be raised to 63, beginning with a lag and phased in over time. The increase in the early retirement age would not be based on the increase in average life expectancy, but rather on the increase in life expectancy for the bottom half of the income distribution, which is substantially lower.

Raising the early retirement age would be unfair to people near retirement, who had based their savings and working plans on the current retirement age of 62. However, raising it with a long lead time and a long phase-in would make sense, given the increase in life expectancy. In addition, while some people have physically demanding jobs, the percentage in those jobs has declined considerably, so, arguably, national retirement age policy should not be based on the small percentage of the workforce in those jobs.

To offset the hardship for some groups that raising the early retirement age would cause, the requirements for Social Security Disability Insurance would be loosened at age 62. In addition, a reform could include the following actions:

- Implement a more aggressive program designed to reduce age discrimination in employment.

- Enact a program of job retraining specifically for older workers.

- Make available extended unemployment benefits for those aged 62–63.

- Increase the normal retirement age, beginning with a lag and being phased in, with the effect being offset for those with low benefits by the minimum benefit.

Another reform would give credit for all work above 38 years through a new benefit. This proposal would create a Notional Defined Contribution (NDC) system for work above 38 years. With that system, each person working more than 38 years would have a notional account to which his payroll tax payments would be credited. The employer's payments would continue to go into the Social Security Trust Fund. Each worker would be credited interest on the account, so the account would appear to workers to be like an individual pension account, but with the difference being that the account would be unfunded. This approach would provide credit for long careers but with no change in the existing benefit formula. The extra taxes they paid would be credited to the NDC system, so they would not be penalized as they currently are for long careers.

An alternative to this proposal is that the accounts could be invested in the Thrift Savings Plan that currently is available only for federal government workers, members of Congress, and the military. For example, they could be invested in the target date fund applicable for the person's age. The worker's contribution would be invested in the Thrift Savings Plan, while the employer's contribution would be sent to the Social Security trust fund. This could be a voluntary option that workers would be informed about, but that they would need to affirmatively choose.

Social Security adjusts benefits for postponed retirement, but over time with the increase in life expectancy at older ages, the adjustment for postponed retirement has become overly generous. Those persons who are able to postpone retirement generally receive higher lifetime benefits. This arrangement disproportionately favors higher-income persons because they are more likely to postpone retirement or to have sufficient resources so that they can retire but postpone when they claim Social Security benefits. Thus, a reform that would improve the financing of Social Security and its equity would reduce the adjustment of benefits for postponed retirement.

FRAMING OR NAMING REFORMS

A minor reform that would lead to less confusion about Social Security is to rename the FICA tax as the Social Security Payroll tax. Other renaming ideas include calling age 62 the early retirement age instead of the Social Security retirement age. Similarly, the full or normal retirement age, currently age 66, is neither full in terms of maximizing benefits nor normal in the statistical sense of most likely. Age 70 should replace age 66 as the full retirement age because that is when postponing receipt no longer increases benefits. If a longevity insurance benefit is added, Social Security Old-Age and Survivors Insurance (OASI) could be renamed Old-Age, Survivors and Longevity Insurance (OASLI).

Automatic Adjustments

A different approach to Social Security reform that recognizes the difficulty of political action during the era of cutbacks involves automatic changes. Congress could pass a law that specifies automatic changes that are tied to factors such as improvement in life expectancy and declines in system solvency. At least a dozen countries, including Japan, Sweden, and Germany, have adopted this approach. A simple automatic adjustment mechanism that would maintain solvency would adjust the normal retirement age upward in line with increases in the old-age dependency ratio. Alternatively, the automatic adjustment could involve both revenue increases and benefit cuts. Or, automatic adjustments could be tied to increases in the life expectancy of people in the bottom half of the income distribution. That measure would show a substantially smaller improvement in life expectancy than would a measure based on the experience of the entire population.

This change would be made to correct for the effect of increased longevity and could be part of a policy for Social Security that systematically adjusted the system to deal with the various effects of increased longevity. A longevity policy for Social Security would improve the reform process; it would help maintain Social Security's solvency by making some changes as technical corrections rather than as politically divisive changes. With a longevity policy, all fixed ages in the Social Security program—the early retirement age, the normal retirement age, the age at which survivors benefits and spousal benefits can be received, and the age at which postponement of retirement no longer leads to higher benefits would periodically be adjusted upward to take into account improvements in life expectancy. In addition, the adjustment of benefits for postponed retirement would be changed to maintain actuarial fairness so that lifetime benefits would be the same whether the person took benefits immediately or postponed receipt.

The exact parameters of the changes in the early and normal retirement ages, tax rates, and taxable maximum ceiling would depend on when the reform was enacted, with smaller changes being needed the sooner the reform is enacted.

CHANGING POLICY DEFAULTS: A SECOND-BEST SOLUTION

Unfortunately, instead of the "ideal" solutions outlined above, Social Security reform could occur at the last moment, with the pressure of a crisis forcing politicians to finally act. Recognizing that the apparent inability of Congress to act in a timely manner is the biggest problem facing Social Security, this book offers an alternative, second-best approach for dealing with the reform process.

Using insights from behavioral economics and the power of defaults, Congress could pass a law that requires it to take action if insolvency is 15 or fewer years away. If it fails to take action within one year of that point, automatic changes involving benefit cuts and tax increases will occur that will restore solvency for the following 20 years. The default changes would provide an incentive for Congress to pass its own reform, which would ensure that action is taken on a reasonably timely basis, and would also reduce the hurdle in that it does not require that solvency be solved for 75 years into the future but only for 20. Thus, instead of Social Security reforms being done as major reforms at the last minute, this approach would facilitate them being done as a series of incremental reforms that can be smaller because they are made in advance.

Ultimately, the reason Congress is not acting on Social Security reform is that no one is pressuring it to do so. Thus, this proposal has one additional part. The Social Security Administration sends out projected benefit statements to people every five years—when they reach ages 25, 30, 35, etc. However, these statements provide misleading information—they provide projected benefits based on the benefit formula in the current law. It is misleading because Social Security is inadequately funded, and unless there is a reform, by law it will provide benefits only at the level that can be paid for—roughly a quarter less. Social Security should amend its benefit statement and provide both the current information and the benefits that will be paid in the absence of reform. This will result in people understanding that they probably will not receive the higher level of benefits, which will likely result in pressure on Congress to act.

ORIGINALISM: RETURNING SOCIAL SECURITY TO ITS ROOTS

Originalism is a principle of legal interpretation that sees the U.S. Constitution as "fixed" as of the time of its enactment. Sometimes policy analysts base arguments for Social Security reform using the same concept—they cite the views of President Franklin D. Roosevelt and aim to return Social Security to the way it was initially conceived, though those arguments tend to be selective as to which elements of Social Security to restore. I do not endorse the principle of originalism and argue instead that reforms should be judged on other grounds discussed in this book. Nonetheless, five reforms that meet both sets of criteria have been discussed in this book.

1) Raise the payroll tax rate so that a higher percentage of total earnings are covered, as in the past.

2) Raise the retirement age to 63 rather than 65.

3) Reinstate a longevity insurance benefit that starts at age 82. When Social Security was first started, it was primarily a longevity insurance benefit program that provided benefits at an age where roughly half of those persons entering the workforce had died. While the language was not used to describe Social Security at the time, that description is consistent with how it actually worked and is consistent with the historical record as to how the age of 65 was selected for retirement benefit eligibility. Now it provides wage-replacement benefits to most people who entered the workforce.

4) Reduce the generosity of the adjustment of benefits for postponed retirement so that the adjustment is actuarially fair, as initially intended. This would save Social Security money and make the system more progressive. When the adjustment factors for calculating benefits with postponed retirement were first put in place, they were actuarially fair, meaning that a person with average life expectancy would receive the equivalent amount in present value of benefits if they delayed receipt of benefits for one year. Now the adjustment factor is generous and rewards those who postpone retirement. The problem is that the people benefiting from this feature are primarily upper-income workers, so the feature has become regressive in that it disproportionately benefits them.

5) Add a caregiver's credit. Social Security originally provided support for caregivers through the spousal benefit. While that benefit is still available, with the increase in

female labor force participation, increasingly, caregivers are receiving benefits in their own right, so that caregivers suffer a loss of Social Security benefits because of their time out of the labor force. Just as the spousal benefit recognizes the important contribution of work taking care of a family in traditional families, a caregiver's credit would be in the spirit of the original Social Security program in that it would recognize the contribution of caregivers in the context of modern families.

THE FINAL WORD

Recognizing the political realities that some people are adamantly opposed to Social Security benefit cuts and others are equally opposed to payroll tax increases, political compromise is clearly needed by both sides. Moreover, we need smart policies that minimize the negative effects of the actions taken.

Policy procrastination by Congress is arguably the biggest problem facing Social Security. It is time for this to end. Making policy changes in 2016, rather than in 2034, will result in fewer benefit cuts or lower payroll tax rate increases. It will also reduce the political risk for workers, Social Security beneficiaries, and employers. The current situation makes it difficult for workers to plan for retirement because of the uncertainty about what their future Social Security benefits will be.

Ultimately, Congress will decide how to reform Social Security, and thus it will be a political decision. The merits and problems with the various options will be weighed in the political context. Thus, the decision of whether to cut benefits or to raise taxes will be based on a political assessment of the effects of these proposals. Many people have expressed concern that a benefit cut would have a large effect on low-income people. That concern can be addressed by making targeted benefit cuts through the benefit formula, rather than through an increase in the normal retirement age, and by having targeted benefit increases.

References

1994–1996 Advisory Council on Social Security. 1996. *Report of the 1994-1996 Advisory Council on Social Security.* Washington, DC: Social Security Advisory Council. https://www.ssa.gov/history/reports/adcouncil/report/toc.htm (accessed May 3, 2016).

Altman, Nancy J. 2015. "Independence Day, Thomas Paine, and Social Security." *The Blog, Huff Post,* July 2. http://www.huffingtonpost.com/nancy-altman/independence-day-thomas-p_b_7715674.html (accessed July 7, 2016).

Altman, Nancy J., and Eric R. Kingson. 2015. *Social Security Works! Why Social Security Isn't Going Broke and How Expanding It Will Help Us All.* New York: New Press.

American Academy of Actuaries. 2002. "Automatic Adjustments to Maintain Social Security's Long-Range Actuarial Balance." Issue Brief. Washington, DC: American Academy of Actuaries.

Arias, Elizabeth. 2014. "United States Life Tables, 2009." *National Vital Statistics Reports* 2(7): 1–62. http://www.cdc.gov/nchs/data/nvsr/nvsr62/nvsr62_07.pdf (accessed April 28, 2016).

Backman, Maurie. 2016. "Here's How Bernie Sanders Plans to Save Social Security." *The Motley Fool,* February 21. http://www.fool.com/investing/general/2016/02/21/heres-how-bernie-sanders-plans-to-save-social-secu.aspx (accessed April 28, 2016).

Baker, Dean, and Nicole Woo. 2014. "The Big Tax Increase That Nobody Noticed." Washington, DC: National Academy of Social Insurance. http://www.nasi.org/discuss/2014/09/big-tax-increase-nobody-noticed (accessed April 28, 2016).

Barr, Nicholas. 1993. *The Economics of the Welfare State,* 2nd ed. Stanford, CA: Stanford University Press.

Bell, Felicitie C., and Michael L. Miller. 2005. "Life Tables for the United States Social Security Area, 1900–2100." Actuarial Study No. 120. Washington, DC: Social Security Administration, Office of the Chief Actuary. http://www.ssa.gov/oact/NOTES/pdf_studies/study120.pdf (accessed April 28, 2016).

Benartzi, Shlomo, and Richard H. Thaler. 2004. "Save More Tomorrow: Using Behavioral Economics to Increase Employee Saving." *Journal of Political Economy* 112(1): S164–S187. http://papers.ssrn.com/sol3/papers.cfm?abstract_id=489693 (accessed April 28, 2016).

Benítez-Silva, H., Berna Demiralp, and Zhen Liu. 2009. "Social Security Literacy and Retirement Well-Being." Working Paper No. 2009-210. Ann Arbor, MI: University of Michigan Retirement Research Center. http://www.mrrc.isr.umich.edu/publications/papers/pdf/wp210.pdf (accessed April 28, 2016).

Biggs, Andrew G., and Sylvester J. Schieber. 2014. "Miscalculating the Retirement Income You'll Need." *Wall Street Journal*, July 15. http://www.wsj.com/articles/miscalculating-the-retirement-income-youll-need -1405380517 (accessed April 28, 2016).

Blake, David, and John A. Turner. 2007. "Individual Accounts for Social Security Reform: Lessons from the United Kingdom." *Benefits Quarterly* 23(3): 56–61.

———. 2014. "Longevity Insurance Annuities: Lessons from the United Kingdom." *Benefits Quarterly* 30(1): 39–47.

Bosworth, Barry, Gary Burtless, and Kan Zhang. 2016. "Later Retirement, Inequality in Old Age, and the Growing Gap in Longevity between Rich and Poor." Washington, DC: Brookings Institution. http://www.brookings .edu/~/media/research/files/reports/2016/01/life-expectancy-gaps -promise-social-security/BosworthBurtlessZhang_retirementinequality longevity_012815.pdf?la=en (accessed April 28, 2016).

Bosworth, Barry, and R. Kent Weaver. 2011. "Social Security on Auto-Pilot: International Experience with Automatic Stabilizer Mechanisms." CRR Working Paper No. 2011-18. Chestnut Hill, MA: Center for Retirement Research at Boston College.

Brady, David, and Craig Volden. 2006. *Revolving Gridlock: Politics and Policy from Jimmy Carter to George W. Bush.* Boulder, CO: Westview Press.

Brandon, Emily, 2014. "5 Potential Social Security Fixes: These Social Security Changes Would Correct the Funding Shortfall." *U.S. News & World Report*, November 14. http://money.usnews.com/money/blogs/planning -to-retire/2014/11/14/5-potential-social-security-fixes (accessed April 28, 2016).

Bridges, Benjamin, and Robert V. Gesumaria. 2013. "The Supplemental Poverty Measure (SPM) and the Aged: How and Why the SPM and Official Poverty Estimates Differ." *Social Security Bulletin* 73(4): 1–69.

Bruce, Ellen A., and John A. Turner. 2003. "Let Lost Retirement Money Revert to Social Security." *Contingencies* May/June: 26–29.

Burkhauser, Richard V., and John A. Turner. 1985. "Is the Social Security Payroll Tax a Tax?" *Public Finance Quarterly* 13(3): 253–267.

Butrica, Barbara A., Howard M. Iams, and Karen E. Smith. 2004. "The Changing Role of Social Security in Retirement Income in the United States." *Social Security Bulletin* 65(3): 1–13.

Canada Pension Plan Investment Board (CPPIB). 2013a. "CPPIB at a Glance: Who We Are." Toronto, ON: CPPIB. http://www.cppib.com/en/who-we -are.html (accessed April 28, 2016).

———. 2013b. "Historical Asset Mix Comparison." Toronto, ON: CPPIB. http://www.cppib.com/en/what-we-do.html (accessed April 28, 2016).

———. 2016. "2015 Annual Report." Toronto, ON: CPPIB. http://www .cppib.com/en/our-performance.html (accessed April 28, 2016).

Center for Retirement Research at Boston College. 2015. "The 2016 Presidential Candidates on Social Security." Chestnut Hill, MA: Center for Retirement Research at Boston College. http://crr.bc.edu/newsroom/featured-work/2016-presidential-candidates-views-on-social-security/ (accessed April 28, 2016).

Centers for Disease Control and Prevention, National Center for Health Statistics, National Vital Statistics System. 2011. "Table 22: Life Expectancy at Birth, at Age 65, and at Age 75 by Sex, Race, and Hispanic Origin: United States, Selected Years 1900–2010." Atlanta, GA: National Center for Health Statistics. http://www.cdc.gov/nchs/data/hus/2011/022.pdf (accessed April 28, 2016).

Chen, Tianhong, Gerard Hughes, and John A. Turner. 2016. "Longevity Insurance Benefits for Social Security: International Experience." *Benefits Quarterly* 32(2): 43–53.

Chen, Tianhong, and John A. Turner. 2014. "Social Security Individual Accounts in China: Sustainability in Individual Account Financing." *Sustainability* 6(8): 5049–5064. doi:10.3390/su6085049 (accessed April 28, 2016).

———. 2015. "Longevity Insurance Annuities: China Adopts a Benefit Innovation from the Past." *International Social Security Review* 68(2): 27–42.

Chen, Yung-Ping, and John A. Turner. 2007. "Raising the Retirement Age in OECD Countries." In *Work Options for Older Americans*, Teresa Ghilarducci and John Turner, eds. New York: Alfred P. Sloan Foundation, pp. 359–369.

Choi, James J., David Laibson, Brigitte Madrian, and Andrew Metrick. 2002. "Defined Contribution Plans: Plan Rules, Participant Choices, and the Path of Least Resistance." In *Tax Policy and the Economy*, Vol. 16. James M. Poterba, ed. Cambridge, MA: MIT Press, pp. 67–113.

Clinton, Hillary. 2016. "Social Security and Medicare." https://www.hillaryclinton.com/issues/social-security-and-medicare (accessed April 28, 2016).

Committee for a Responsible Federal Budget. 2013. "Social Security Reform and the Cost of Delay." Washington, DC: Committee for a Responsible Federal Budget. http://crfb.org/sites/default/files/social_security_cost_of_waiting_8_22_13.pdf (accessed April 28, 2016).

Congressional Budget Office. 2015a. "The 2015 Long-Term Budget Outlook." Washington, DC: Congressional Budget Office. http://www.cbo.gov/publication/50250 (accessed April 28, 2016).

———. 2015b. "Social Security Policy Options, 2015." Washington, DC: Congressional Budget Office. https://www.cbo.gov/sites/default/files/114th-congress-2015-2016/reports/51011-SSOptions_OneCol.pdf (accessed April 28, 2016).

Craver, Martha Lynn. 2015. "Big Changes Coming for Medicare, Social Security?" *Washington Matters* (blog), *Kiplinger*, June 19. http://www .kiplinger.com/article/business/T043-C012-S003-big-changes-coming -for-medicare-social-security.html (accessed April 28, 2016).

Diamond, Peter A., and Peter R. Orszag. 2004. *Saving Social Security: A Balanced Approach.* Washington, DC: Brookings Institution.

Doescher, Tabitha, and John A. Turner. 1988. "Social Security Benefits and the Baby Boom Generation." *American Economic Review* 78(2): 76–80.

Employee Benefits Research Institute (EBRI). 2015. "Attitudes about Current Social Security and Medicare Benefit Levels." RCS Fact Sheet No. 6. Washington, DC: EBRI. http://www.ebri.org/files/RCS15.FS-6 .Entitlmnts2.pdf (accessed April 29, 2016).

Garabato, Natalia. 2016. "Why Workers Retire When They Do: A Survey of U.S. Retirees." Towers Watson, January 27. https://www.towerswatson .com/en/Insights/Newsletters/Americas/insider/2016/01/why-workers -retire-when-they-do-a-survey-of-u-s-retirees (accessed May 3, 2016).

Ghilarducci, Teresa, and John Turner, eds. 2007. *Work Options for Older Americans.* Notre Dame, IN: University of Notre Dame.

Gillion, Colin, John A. Turner, Clive Bailey, and Denis Latulippe, eds. 2000. *Social Security Pensions: Development and Reform.* Geneva: International Labor Office.

Glover, James W. 1921. "United States Life Tables: 1890, 1901, 1910, and 1901–1910." Washington, DC: U.S. Bureau of the Census, U.S. Government Printing Office. http://www.cdc.gov/nchs/data/lifetables/life1890 -1910.pdf (accessed April 29, 2016).

Goss, Stephen C. 2016. "Letter to the Honorable Bernie Sanders." Washington, DC: Social Security Administration, Office of the Chief Actuary. https://www.socialsecurity.gov/OACT/solvency/index.html (accessed April 29, 2016).

Goss, Stephen C., Alice H. Wade, and Christopher J. Chaplain. 2008. "Estimated Financial Effects of 'A Reform Proposal to Make Social Security Financially Sound, Fairer, and More Progressive' by Mark Warshawsky." Washington, DC: Social Security Administration, Office of the Chief Actuary. https://www.socialsecurity.gov/OACT/solvency/ Warshawsky_20080917.pdf (accessed April 29, 2016).

Government of the United Kingdom. 2016. "Voluntary National Insurance Contributions." London: Government of the United Kingdom. https:// www.gov.uk/voluntary-national-insurance-contributions (accessed April 29, 2016).

Hayashi, Yuka. 2012. "Japan's Social Security Reforms—A History of Inaction." *JapanRealTime* (blog), *Wall Street Journal*, August 13. http://blogs .wsj.com/japanrealtime/2012/08/13/japans-social-security-reform-a -history-of-inaction/ (accessed April 29, 2016).

Henriques, Alice M. 2012. "How Does Social Security Claiming Respond to Incentives? Considering Husbands' and Wives' Benefits Separately." Working Paper No. 2012-19. Washington, DC: Board of Governors of the Federal Reserve System.

Holzmann, Robert, and Joseph E. Stiglitz. 2001. *New Ideas about Old Age Security.* Washington, DC: World Bank.

Hoskins, Dalmer D. 2010. "U.S. Social Security at 75 Years: An International Perspective." *Social Security Bulletin* 70(3): 1–87.

Hughes, Gerard, and John A. Turner. 2015. "Demographic Change and Longevity Insurance Benefits for Public Pension Reform." *Demographic Change and Public Pensions,* in English and Polish, Marek Szczepański, ed. Poznan, Poland: Poznan University Press.

Hurd, Michael D., and Susann Rohwedder. 2015. "Measuring Economic Preparation for Retirement: Income versus Consumption." Working Paper No. 2015-332. Ann Arbor, MI: Michigan Center for Retirement Research.

Investment Company Institute. 2015. "Investment Company Factbook 2015." Washington, DC: Investment Company Institute. https://www.ici.org/pdf/2015_factbook.pdf (accessed April 29, 2016).

Iwry, J. Mark, and John A. Turner. 2009. "New Behavioral Strategies for Expanding Lifetime Income in 401(k)s." In *Automatic: Changing the Way America Saves,* William G. Gale, J. Mark Iwry, David John, and Lina Walker, eds. Washington, DC: Brookings Institution, pp. 151–172.

Johnson, Richard W. 2004. "Trends in Job Demands among Older Workers: 1992–2002." *Monthly Labor Review* 127(7): 48–56.

Kritzer, Barbara E., and Barbara A. Smith. 2016. "Public Pension Statements in Selected Countries: A Comparison." *Social Security Bulletin* 76(1): 1–56.

Kwena, Rose Musonye, and John A. Turner. 2013. "Extending Pension and Savings Scheme Coverage to the Informal Sector: Kenya's Mbao Pension Plan." *International Social Security Review* 66(2): 79–99.

Lachowska, Marta, and Michal Myck. 2015. "What Is the Relation between Public Pensions and Private Savings?" *Employment Research* 22(3): 1–3. http://research.upjohn.org/empl_research/vol22/iss3/1 (accessed July 7, 2016).

Lichtenstein, Jules H., and John A. Turner. 2002. "Social Security Reform in the Middle East: A Brief Review." *Aging and Social Policy* 14(1): 115–124.

Leibman, Jeffrey, Maya MacGuineas, and Andrew Samwick. 2005. "Nonpartisan Social Security Reform Plan." Hanover, NH: Dartmouth College. http://www.dartmouth.edu/~samwick/lms_nonpartisan_plan_description.pdf (accessed August 4, 2016).

Light, Paul C. 2005. "The Crisis Last Time: Social Security Reform." Washington, DC: Brookings Institution. http://www.brookings.edu/research/opinions/2005/03/05saving-light (accessed May 3, 2016).

Lind, Michael, Joshua Freedman, Steven Hill, and Robert Hiltonsmith. 2013. "Expanding Social Security." New York: New America Foundation. http://www.newamerica.net/publications/policy/expanded_social_security (accessed May 3, 2016).

Liu, Lillian. 2000. "Public Pension Reform in Japan." *Social Security Bulletin* 63(4): 99–106.

Luttmer, Erzo F.P., and Andrew A. Samwick. 2015. "The Welfare Cost of Perceived Policy Uncertainty: Evidence from Social Security." Unpublished paper. National Bureau of Economic Research, Cambridge, MA. http://users.nber.org/~luttmer/polrisk_paper.pdf (accessed May 3, 2016).

Madrian, Brigitte C., and Dennis Shea. 2001. "The Power of Suggestion: Inertia in 401(k) Participation and Savings Behavior." *Quarterly Journal of Economics* 116(4): 1149–1187.

Maurer, Raimond, Olivia S. Mitchell, Ralf Rogala, and Tatjana Schimetschek. 2016. "The Potential Effect of Offering Lump Sums in the Social Security Program." *Public Policy Initiative* 3(9): 1–5.

Mermin, Gordon B., and C. Eugene Steuerle. 2007. "Would Raising the Social Security Retirement Age Harm Lower-Income Groups?" Brief Series, No. 19. Urban Institute, January 30. http://www.urban.org/research/publication/would-raising-social-security-retirement-age-harm-low-income-groups (accessed May 3, 2016).

Meyerson, Noah, and Sheila Dacey. 2013. "How Does Social Security Work?" CBO blog, September 19. Washington, DC: Congressional Budget Office. https://www.cbo.gov/publication/44590 (accessed May 3, 2016).

Mitchell, Olivia S., and John A. Turner. 2010. "Labor Market Uncertainty and Pension System Performance." In *Performance of Privately Managed Pension Funds*, Richard P. Hinz, Heinz P. Rudolf, Pablo Antolin, and Juan Yermo, eds. Washington, DC: World Bank, pp. 119–158.

Monk, Courtney, John A. Turner, and Natalia Zhivan. 2010. "Adjusting Social Security for Increasing Life Expectancy: Effects on Progressivity." CRR Working Paper No. 2010-9. Chestnut Hill, MA: Center for Retirement Research at Boston College.

Muir, Dana M., and John A. Turner. 2011. *Imagining the Ideal Pension System*. Kalamazoo, MI: W.E. Upjohn Institute for Employment Research.

Muller, Leslie A., and John A. Turner. 2013. "The Persistence of Employee 401(k) Contributions over a Major Stock Market Cycle: The Limited Power of Inertia." *Benefits Quarterly* 29(3): 51–65.

Muller, Leslie A., Adelin Levin, and John A. Turner. 2016. "Survivorship Bias Due to Differential Mortality: A New Measure of Old-Age Poverty." Pension Policy Center Working Paper No. 2016-03. Washington, DC: Pension Policy Center.

Munnell, Alicia H. 2013. "Social Security Should Own Equities." *Market-Watch* (blog), *Marketwatch*, March 20. http://blogs.marketwatch.com/encore/2013/03/20/social-security-should-own-equities/ (accessed May 3, 2016).

Munnell, Alicia H., and Anqi Chen. 2015. "Trends in Social Security Claiming." Issue Brief 15-8. Chestnut Hill, MA: Center for Retirement Research at Boston College.

Munnell, Alicia H., and Steven A. Sass. 2006. *Social Security and the Stock Market: How the Pursuit of Market Magic Shapes the System.* Kalamazoo, MI: W.E. Upjohn Institute for Employment Research.

———. 2008. *Working Longer: The Solution to the Retirement Income Challenge.* Washington, DC: Brookings Institution.

National Academies of Sciences, Engineering, and Medicine. 2015. *The Growing Gap in Life Expectancy by Income: Implications for Federal Programs and Policy Responses.* Washington, DC: National Academies Press.

Niu, Xiaotong, and Julie Topoleski. 2014. "What Are the Causes of Projected Growth in Spending for Social Security and Major Health Care Programs?" CBO blog, July 18. Washington, DC: Congressional Budget Office. https://www.cbo.gov/publication/45543 (accessed May 3, 2016).

Organisation for Economic Co-operation and Development (OECD). 2015. *Pensions at a Glance: OECD and G20 Indicators.* Paris: OECD.

Office of Management and Budget. 2013. "Chained CPI Protections." Fact sheet. Washington, DC: Office of Management and Budget.

Office of the Superintendent of Financial Institutions. 2013. *Actuarial Report (26th) on the Canada Pension Plan.* Ottawa, ON: Government of Canada.

Palmer, Edward. 2000. "The Swedish Pension Reform Model: Framework and Issues." Social Protection Discussion Paper No. 0012. Washington, DC: World Bank.

Penner, Rudolph G., and C. Eugene Steuerle. 2007. "Stabilizing Future Fiscal Policy: It's Time to Pull the Trigger." Washington, DC: Urban Institute.

Peterson, Jonathan. 2015. "Securing the Future: 3 Reasons Why Social Security Will Be There for You." *AARP Bulletin* July/August: 18–20.

Reno, Virginia P., and David John. 2012. "Option: Cover All Newly Hired State and Local Government Workers." *Perspectives* 27(June). http://www.aarp.org/content/dam/aarp/research/public_policy_institute/econ_sec/2012/option-cover-all-newly-hired-government-workers-AARP-ppi-econ-sec.pdf (accessed June 2, 2016).

Reno, Virginia P., and Elisa A. Walker. 2013. "Social Security Benefits, Finances, and Policy Options: A Primer." Washington, DC: National Academy of Social Insurance. http://www.nasi.org/sites/default/files/research/2013_Social_Security_Primer_PDF.pdf (accessed June 2, 2016).

Samborski, Adam, and John A. Turner. 2015. "Complexity in Risks Facing Pension Plans: Nonmarket Financial Risk in the United States and Poland." *Journal of Economics and Management* 21(3): 35–57.

Sarney, Mark. 2008. "Distributional Effects of Increasing the Benefit Computation Period." Social Security Policy Brief No. 2008-02. Washington, DC: Social Security Administration. http://www.socialsecurity.gov/policy/docs/policybriefs/pb2008-02.pdf (accessed June 2, 2016).

Schieber, Sylvester J. 2012. *The Predictable Surprise: The Unraveling of the U.S. Retirement System.* Oxford and New York: Oxford University Press.

Schieber, Sylvester J., and John B. Shoven. 1999. *The Real Deal: The History and Future of Social Security.* New Haven, CT: Yale University Press.

Shen, Sally, and John A. Turner. 2016. "Analyzing the Quality of Financial Advice: Do Conflicted Advisers Tell Half Truths?" Pension Policy Center Working Paper No. 2016-04. Washington, DC: Pension Policy Center.

Social Security Administration. 2014. "Social Security Basic Facts." http://www.ssa.gov/news/press/basicfact.html. Washington, DC: Social Security Administration.

———. 2016a. "Age 65 Retirement." Washington, DC: Social Security Administration. https://www.ssa.gov/history/age65.html (accessed June 2, 2016).

———. 2016b. "Effective Interest Rates." Washington, DC: Social Security Administration. https://www.ssa.gov/OACT/ProgData/effectiveRates.html (accessed June 2, 2016).

Social Security Office of the Chief Actuary. 2013. "Letter to the Honorable Sam Johnson, Chairman, Subcommittee on Social Security, Committee on Ways and Means, House of Representatives." Washington, DC: Social Security Office of the Chief Actuary.

Social Security Trustees. 2008. *The 2008 OASDI Trustees Report.* Washington, DC: Social Security Administration. https://www.ssa.gov/oact/tr/tr08/trtoc.html (accessed July 7, 2016).

———. 2013. *The 2013 Annual Report of the Board of Trustees of the Federal Old-Age and Survivors Insurance and Federal Disability Insurance Trust Funds.* Washington, DC: Social Security Administration.

———. 2014. *A Summary of the 2014 Annual Reports.* http://www.ssa.gov/oact/trsum/index.html. Washington, DC: Social Security Administration.

Steuerle, Eugene, and Jon M. Bakija. 1994. *Retooling Social Security for the 21st Century: Right & Wrong Approaches to Reform.* Washington, DC: Urban Institute Press.

———. 2015. *The 2015 Annual Report of the Board of Trustees of the Federal Old-Age and Survivors Insurance and Federal Disability Insurance Trust Funds.* Washington, DC: Social Security Administration. http://www.ssa.gov/oact/tr/2015/tr2015.pdf (accessed April 28, 2016).

Stinson, Sonya. 2015. "Can Social Security Be Garnished?" Bankrate, June 1. http://www.bankrate.com/finance/retirement/social-security-garnished-1.aspx (accessed May 3, 2016).

Sullivan, Tim. 2016. "Budget Bill Brings Major Social Security Changes for Some." *Columbia Daily Tribune*, February 20. http://www.columbiatribune.com/business/saturday_business/budget-bill-brings-major-social-security-changes-for-some/article_7741eba5-a368-5f7a-8bcf-1c19b72e1672.html (accessed May 3, 2016).

Szczepański, Marek, and John A. Turner, eds. 2014a. *Social Security and Pension Reform: International Perspectives.* Kalamazoo, MI: W.E. Upjohn Institute for Employment Research.

_____. 2014b. "Social Security and Pension Reform: The Views of Sixteen Authors." In *Social Security and Pension Reform: International Perspectives*, Marek Szczepański and John A. Turner, eds. Kalamazoo, MI: W.E. Upjohn Institute for Employment Research, pp. 3–12.

Thompson, Lawrence H. 1998. *Older and Wiser: The Economics of Public Pensions.* Washington, DC: Urban Institute Press.

Turner, John A. 1984. "Population Age Structure and the Size of Social Security." *Southern Economic Journal* 50(April): 1131–1146.

———, ed. 2001. *Pay at Risk: Risk Bearing by U.S. and Canadian Workers.* Kalamazoo, MI: W.E. Upjohn Institute for Employment Research.

———. 2004. "Individual Accounts: Lessons from Sweden." *International Social Security Review* 57(1): 65–84.

———. 2006. *Individual Accounts for Social Security Reform: International Perspectives on the U.S. Debate.* Kalamazoo, MI: W.E. Upjohn Institute for Employment Research.

———. 2007. "Social Security Pensionable Ages in OECD Countries: 1949–2035." *International Social Security Review* 60(1): 81–99.

———. 2010. *Pension Policy—The Search for Better Solutions.* Kalamazoo, MI: W.E. Upjohn Institute for Employment Research.

———. 2011. *Longevity Policy: Facing Up to Longevity Issues Affecting Social Security, Pensions, and Older Workers.* Kalamazoo, MI: W.E. Upjohn Institute for Employment Research.

———. 2013. "Providing Longevity Insurance Annuities: A Comparison of the Private Sector versus Social Security." *Journal of Retirement* 1(2): 125–130.

Turner, John A., and Bruce W. Klein. 2016. "Modernizing Pension Eligibility for the U.S. Military." *Journal of Retirement* 3(3): 116–127.

Turner, John A., Bruce W. Klein, and Norman P. Stein. 2016. "Financial Illiteracy Meets Conflicted Advice: The Case of Thrift Savings Plan Rollovers." Pension Policy Center Working Paper No. 2016-02. Washington, DC: Pension Policy Center.

Turner, John A., and David D. McCarthy. 2013. "Longevity Insurance Annuities in 401(k) Plans and IRAs." *Benefits Quarterly* 29(1): 58–62.

Turner, John A., and David M. Rajnes. 2016. "Evolving Social Security Systems in Four Countries: Relevant Trends for the United States." Pension Policy Center Working Paper No. 2016-01. Washington, DC: Pension Policy Center.

Turner, John A., Noriyasu Watanabe, and David M. Rajnes. 1994. "'Pay or Play' Pensions in Japan." *Contingencies* (Nov./Dec.): 63–65.

Waldron, Hilary. 2007. "Trends in Mortality Differentials and Life Expectancy for Male Social Security–Covered Workers, by Socioeconomic Status." *Social Security Bulletin* 67(3): 1–28.

———. 2013. "Mortality Differentials by Lifetime Earnings Decile: Implications for Evaluations of Proposed Social Security Law Changes." *Social Security Bulletin* 73(1): 1–37.

Wall Street Journal. 2015. "Who's Rich Enough to See Social Security Cuts under Chris Christie's Plan?" April 20. http://blogs.wsj.com/economics/ 2015/04/20/whos-rich-enough-to-see-social-security-cuts-under-chris -christies-plan (accessed June 2, 2016).

Weaver, Kent, and Alexander Willén. 2014. "The Swedish Pension System after Twenty Years: Mid-course Corrections and Lessons." *OECD Journal on Budgeting* 13(3): 1–26.

Weller, Christian E. 2016. *Retirement on the Rocks: Why Americans Can't Get Ahead and How New Savings Policies Can Help.* New York: Palgrave Macmillan.

Wu, Ke Bin. 2013. "Income and Poverty of Older Americans, 2011." Fact Sheet 287. Washington, DC: AARP Public Policy Institute. http://www .aarp.org/content/dam/aarp/research/public_policy_institute/econ _sec/2013/income-and-poverty-of-older-americans-AARP-ppi-econ-sec .pdf (accessed June 2, 2016).

Author

John A. Turner is director of the Pension Policy Center. He is the former deputy director of the pension research office at the U.S. Department of Labor, and he has taught as an adjunct lecturer in economics at George Washington University. He has published 14 books and more than 100 articles. He and a coauthor received an award for the best article of the year in the *Journal of Risk and Insurance*, and he received the Department of Labor Special Act Award for work preparing the secretary of labor's *Labor Day Report*. Two of Turner's books have been translated into Japanese and three have been required reading for examinations of the Society of Actuaries. Turner is the author of four previous books for the Upjohn Institute, including *Pension Policy: The Search for Better Solutions* in 2010. He has a PhD in economics from the University of Chicago.

Index

The italic letters *n* or *t* following a page number indicate a note or table on that page.

About the Institute

The W.E. Upjohn Institute for Employment Research is a nonprofit research organization devoted to finding and promoting solutions to employment-related problems at the national, state, and local levels. It is an activity of the W.E. Upjohn Unemployment Trustee Corporation, which was established in 1932 to administer a fund set aside by Dr. W.E. Upjohn, founder of The Upjohn Company, to seek ways to counteract the loss of employment income during economic downturns.

The Institute is funded largely by income from the W.E. Upjohn Unemployment Trust, supplemented by outside grants, contracts, and sales of publications. Activities of the Institute comprise the following elements: 1) a research program conducted by a resident staff of professional social scientists; 2) a competitive grant program, which expands and complements the internal research program by providing financial support to researchers outside the Institute; 3) a publications program, which provides the major vehicle for disseminating the research of staff and grantees, as well as other selected works in the field; and 4) an Employment Management Services division, which manages most of the publicly funded employment and training programs in the local area.

The broad objectives of the Institute's research, grant, and publication programs are to 1) promote scholarship and experimentation on issues of public and private employment and unemployment policy, and 2) make knowledge and scholarship relevant and useful to policymakers in their pursuit of solutions to employment and unemployment problems.

Current areas of concentration for these programs include causes, consequences, and measures to alleviate unemployment; social insurance and income maintenance programs; compensation; workforce quality; work arrangements; family labor issues; labor-management relations; and regional economic development and local labor markets.